# THE BOOK:

*Why the First Books of the Bible Were Written
and Who They Were Written For*

## ALLEN WRIGHT

iUniverse, Inc.
Bloomington

iUniverse books may be ordered through booksellers or by contacting:

iUniverse
1663 Liberty Drive
Bloomington, IN 47403
www.iuniverse.com
1-800-Authors (1-800-288-4677)

Because of the dynamic nature of the Internet, any web addresses or links contained in
this book may have changed since publication and may no longer be valid. The views
expressed in this work are solely those of the author and do not necessarily reflect the
views of the publisher, and the publisher hereby disclaims any responsibility for them.

Any people depicted in stock imagery provided by Thinkstock are models,
and such images are being used for illustrative purposes only.

Certain stock imagery © Thinkstock.

ISBN: 978-1-4759-7242-9 (hc)
ISBN: 978-1-4759-7241-2 (sc)
ISBN: 978-1-4759-7243-6 (e)

Library of Congress Control Number: 2013901018

Printed in the United States of America

iUniverse rev. date: 2/15/2013

This book is dedicated to my wonderful and loving mother, Bertha May Mack, who lost her battle with cancer at the age of sixty-two, but not before raising a family of four who had made her proud.

# TABLE OF CONTENTS

# ACKNOWLEDGMENTS

I would first like to thank Dr. Serge Frolov, professor of religion at Southern Methodist University, for his assistance with determining the most accurate and precise dating estimates for the compositions of the biblical books Genesis through Kings II. Specifically, I would like to site Mr. Frolov's "Evil-Merodach and the Deuteronomist: The Sociohistorical Setting of Dtr in the Light of 2 Kgs 25,27-30," *Biblica* 88 (2007), pp. 174-90

I also thank the many excellent history professors at the University of California–Santa Barbara, who long ago instilled within me a lifelong appreciation for history and historical research and methodology during my four great and formative undergraduate years, which culminated in 1975.

I would also like to thank my roommate at UCSB, Jeff Mitcherling (now a professor of philosophy at Guelph University in Guelph, Ontario) for our many excellent conversations regarding history, philosophy, science, and many other topics—and especially for encouraging me to pursue historical research and writing.

Finally, I would like to thank my wife, B. Sue Wright, for her unselfish support during all the hours I put into writing this book.

CHAPTER 1

# Introduction

With this book, I will lead you where my mind and dedicated research led me: to a wonderful, insightful, interesting, and fresh interpretation of the first Bible books to have been written, Genesis through Kings II. While doing so, I will transport you back in time to the ancient period and place of this extraordinary event, the writing of the first books of the Bible. You will return to modern life with a more enlightened understanding of the Bible's first books.

This book is about the Bible. Because the Bible and religion are often seemingly inseparable, one may readily jump to the conclusion that *The Book: Why the First Books of the Bible Were Written and Who They Were Written For* is about religion. It is not. It is about the Bible, its original intended purpose, and its original intended audience. It is also about history and the fascinating long-ago civilizations of the ancient Near East. More important, it's about seeing the Bible through a different lens—one offering a fresh perspective on the Bible that is well worth considering. What you learn by reading this book may disturb you, or it may not. It may challenge your beliefs, or it may not. What I most sincerely hope is that this book will educate, entertain, and enlighten you.

If ever one ubiquitous, omnipresent book has tracked our Western civilization from long before the fall of Rome to the present day, it is the Bible. The Bible, in one form or another, is the written constitution of the most venerable Western institutions in history, the synagogue and the church. More so, the Bible has been revered as a personal constitution among the countless faithful throughout the ages to this day. The Bible has been printed in nearly every language spoken throughout the world. Many have become heirlooms passed down in unbroken chains from one generation to the next. In short, Bibles are found all over the world and in nearly every home in the West. Just about every man, woman, and child knows what the Bible is and something of what it's about.

Surprisingly, just a very few exceedingly rare scraps of biblical writings have been found on parchment in their original ancient Hebrew script. Only a few samples survived, most found among the so-called Dead Sea Scrolls at Khirbet Qumran, off the northwest shore of the Dead Sea, and an even older preserved sample located near ancient Judea. These scraps of writing are beyond priceless; for many, they are the most sacred items on our planet. For biblical scholars, they're something akin.

Given the nearly complete absence of biblical writings in their original ancient Hebrew script, the Bible may well have been lost forever had it not been for a very fortuitous translation into Greek. Consequently, this translation became legendary not long after its completion, and indeed, biblical historians credit the Septuagint, the Greek translation of the Bible, as one of the greatest events of all time and consequently wrapped in legend.

The story of the translation, as told in a book by Aristeas

of Alexandria, was connected with a fanciful miracle, a literary device often used in ancient Hebrew writings and many before them. According to the legend, seventy wise and learned Hebrew scribes traveled to Egypt after Greek-speaking Jews living in Egypt convinced an Egyptian leader to include the books of Moses in his library. When they arrived, as the legend goes, the Egyptian leader placed each one of them into separate rooms to individually translate the writings into Greek. The king then compared the translations, and behold, not a single difference was found among the seventy translations. The Greek word for seventy is *septuagint*, and the Greek translation of the Bible has been known by that name ever since.

Despite the legend attached to the Greek translation, this translation is and always has been considered by nearly all to be a precise and reliable duplication of the original, ancient Hebrew Bible. Any translational subtleties between the original Hebrew script, the Greek Septuagint, and the subsequent King James translation into English (yet another significant biblical historical event) are inconsequential despite many of the feisty arguments made by individuals holding fast onto pure orthodoxy.

## DATING THE BIBLE

Dating is a crucial part of history and historical analysis, needless to say. Many readers today are familiar with the designation BC, meaning Before Christ, and AD, meaning After Christ. The use of these religious connotations, BC and AD, is understandably a sensitive issue for many historians who lack any desire to be insensitive one way or the other toward all parties, believers and nonbelievers alike. In response to this concern, alternative dating designations have been developed. Some like the idea of using BP, or Before Present, meaning simply "ago." In other words, this or that happened 40, 200, or 3,180 years ago, or BP. Of course, the obvious problem with the BP designation is that "years ago" changes. One may read a book three hundred years after its publication that refers to an event as having occurred "300 BP," but this event would have occurred six hundred years ago, or 600 BP, at the time this individual was reading the book.

Given the sensitivities of some, and the long duration of the use of, and familiarity with, the BC and AD dating designations that delineate a before and after period relating to the specific but presumed birthdate of Christ, the more recent dating designations BCE (Before the Common Era) and CE (Common Era), which correspond precisely with BC and AD, are commonly used by many historians and religious scholars today.

This book uses the BCE and CE dating designations and accepts the flaw inherited from the BC and AD dating system—that flaw being the absence of year zero. "Zero" was a numerical or counting concept developed after the BC/AD dating designations came into use. The problem is that AD begins with year one after Christ (1 AD) and counts forward from there, omitting the twelve months leading up to year one. In most cases, ancient Near East history professors do not care what dating designation their students use, as long as they get their dates correct.

## CHAPTER 2

# In the Beginning

The greatest show on earth, humankind, saw its first urban civilization arise between two rivers, the Tigris and Euphrates, around 5,500 BCE (or some 7,500 years ago) in ancient Mesopotamia, near present-day Iraq. Yet, long before this civilization arose, as archaeological finds of early human artifacts reveal, mankind had practiced some form of religion holding notions about some form of higher being or beings possessing a great force.

This is a very reasonable conclusion when one simply looks over the horizon or up into the nighttime sky, sees something we humans didn't put there, and naturally wonders who did. It's a question that begs itself, sparking little surprise that all human societies for at least a good 30,000 years have tried to explain it in some form or fashion.

Eventually, these fascinating views of the curious and dark nighttime sky full of stars sparked inspirational and entertaining talk around the campfire that eventually turned into stories. Their stories became organic, took on a life of their own and grew. In time, these ancient explanations became matters of belief—belief in powerful gods—and around these beliefs and gods religions have formed, grown, matured, blossomed and have been around us ever since. Among the most enduring and most widely accepted organized religions today are the Abrahamic religions, arguably the most influential and historically significant religions found in human history to date. They include the Muslim, Judaic, and Christian faiths, which rest upon the writings that comprise the Quran, Hebrew Bible, and the Old and New Testaments of the Christian Bible.

The Bible's preeminence is due in large part to a popular perception held through the ages: it is seen as speaking the ultimate truth handed down to man by the Lord Himself, which is to say the Bible is perceived as divine. Its infallibility must be strongly embraced, widely accepted, and passionately defended, just as it has among the multitudes for many, many hundreds of years. Accordingly, the Bible has been more collectively read, worshipped, revered, quoted, and studied than any other book. If there is one book, one title that nearly everyone living today is aware of, it's the Bible, a work often referred to as "the greatest story ever told." And indeed, this single literary source has arguably altered and shaped Western history more than any war, any government, any struggle, any calamity, or any popular movement combined.

However, what truly brought the Bible and its compositions into existence was something much closer to home, and what it became is something far, far greater than what it was originally intended to be. Nevertheless, the true story behind the writing of the Bible is indeed one of remarkably great heroes whose names we do not know nor ever will. Those who originated the Bible's first compositions were great and unselfish humanitarians who possessed an unbridled human compassion for their people. It was their work and dedication that is the true and magnificent story behind the story.

This book recounts how these heroes went about saving their own civilization against overwhelming odds—and succeeding. This book will clearly illustrate why the Bible came to be written as it was, and for whom it was written.

The setting of the extraordinary and profound historical event of the Bible's first composition was the ancient Near East. Here, the world's first great human civilizations rose, thrived, declined, and fell, but not before leaving their many wonders for all the generations to come on every corner of the earth to appreciate, ponder, and study. Among these wonders are such splendid treasures as the pyramids and alphabets; laws and philosophy; decorative ornaments; and other abundant architectural and engineering marvels of human achievement. The ancient Near East civilizations comprise many of the grandest civilizations of all, including Mesopotamia, Assyria, Egypt, Persia, Babylonia, and Phoenicia. Smaller and lesser-known civilizations that are also worthy to note include the Hittites and Lydia.

Nestled among these magnificent civilizations was a great paradox, the ancient Hebrews. On one hand, they were an insignificant people compared in all ways to the many civilizations that surrounded them. In another way, with help from the Phoenicians' pioneering alphabet, the Hebrews' influence upon the modern world was longer lasting and farther reaching than all the others combined. Had a group of Hebrews not written the Bible, what would be left of them except a footnote in ancient Near East history textbooks? And had it not been for a series of events and other coincidences, the Bible as we know it would never have been written, and Western and Middle-Eastern history as we know it today would be far different. Was it all just an accident, or was it not? Is there purpose, or do things just happen? This much is for sure: all events have consequences—some small, some large.

The Bible's composition was influenced in two ways, one small the other large. In Part One, you'll clearly see how important stories in the Bible were influenced by extra-biblical, preexisting Mesopotamian literary texts written long before the biblical writers first sat down to the their task. In Part Two, you will see unequivocally how earthly, human events brought the Bible's compositions into existence as a specific human response to adverse events weighing heavily upon the Hebrew people for whom it was written.

CHAPTER 3

# Intertextuality, Case One
## THE DELUGE

The biblical writing project began with the compositions of the Bible's first books, Genesis through Kings II, as they still appear today. The project was undertaken and completed during a two-year period, 562–560 BCE. (In future chapters, you'll see how this precise period has been reasonably narrowed down to this specific time frame.) The remaining books found in the Old Testament (and of course the New Testament) were added over the decades and centuries that followed.

Genesis–Kings II was the result of closely coordinated work among several participating authors. A key significant event leading to the Bible's first composition occurred in 586 BCE following the defeat of the Hebrews and the subsequent sacking of Jerusalem and the destruction of their temple by the Babylonians (an important event you'll read more of in future chapters). The writing of Genesis–Kings II was a direct response to this earthly, historical occurrence, which adversely and severely impacted the writers' fellow Hebrew people. The primary focus of this book is a book-by-book analysis of Genesis through Kings II, found in Part Two, that will clearly illustrate this interpretation of the Bible's first compositions.

While these events weighed large upon the Bible's creation and composition, as you will see, a second and less influential, but very interesting, source of biblical text was the literature of other Near East civilizations, primarily ancient Mesopotamia and, to a lesser extent, Egypt.

Scholars often use the term "intertextuality" when describing text from one source that has found its way into another book or composition, either verbatim or in slightly altered form. This chapter illustrates two examples of intertextuality found in the Bible, but more can be found if one desires to dig deeper. The term *intertextuality* may seem to some to have been invented as a benign word for *plagiarism*, a term defined as "presenting the ideas and words as one's own." Use the word as you may.

The first example of intertextuality can be found by comparing text from the popular story of Noah's ark, which appears in Genesis, with a text found in a much earlier and fascinating literary work known as The Epic of Gilgamesh. The Epic of Gilgamesh was first discovered in the mid-nineteenth century by archaeologists working and digging near present-day Iraq, where the ancient Mesopotamian civilization emerged around 5,500 BCE. The story is of Mesopotamian origin and was found written on stone tablets in cuneiform. Cuneiform was an early form of writing that predated the Phoenician alphabet from which the ancient Hebrew alphabet was derived, along with the alphabets of many other languages. As is commonly known, the Bible was originally written in ancient Hebrew script.

A second example of intertextuality is found in Samuel I's treatment of the popular and familiar duel between David and Goliath. A comparative illustration will show that this popular story of a boy battling a giant resulted from the alteration of several details of an earlier Mesopotamian text, yielding a new version with interesting and revealing changes.

As previously mentioned, very few examples of biblical verse written in Hebrew script prior to the Common Era have been found, and nearly all were among the so-called Dead Sea Scrolls. These priceless artifacts were discovered at Khirbet Qumran and became an archaeological treasure trove. Among these ancient Hebrew remains were biblical verses written in their original Hebrew script and dated between 2 BCE and 1 CE. Had it not been for the wisdom and work of the ancient Jewish historian Josephus, whose foresight and urging prompted the Hebrew Bible to be translated into Greek, the entire work best known today as the Old Testament may have easily been lost forever, as evidenced by the near complete absence today of any surviving Hebrew biblical script written before the Common Era. The frequent upheaval of the Jewish people throughout their early history placed a large strain on the preservation of their limited collections of sacred but balky scrolls through the ages.

Included with, or later inserted into the text of, the ancient literary masterpiece The Epic of Gilgamesh is a chapter titled "The Deluge," or "The Flood." Again, be reminded this was written in cuneiform long before the Phoenician Hebrew alphabet was configured. Read that short story from The Epic of Gilgamesh below, and then immediately compare it with the biblical story of Noah. I find it very interesting, though some might find it disturbing:

1. The dates of 562–560 BCE for the composition of Genesis–Kings II were carefully calculated by Dr. Serge Frolov of Southern Methodist University's department of religion, with whom I agree.

## THE STORY OF THE FLOOD

'You know the city Shurrupak; it stands on the banks of Euphrates? That city grew old and the gods that were in it were old. There was Anu, lord of the firmament, their father, and warrior Enlil their counselor, Ninurta the helper, and Ennugi watcher over canals; and with them also was Ea. In those days the world teemed, the people multiplied, the world bellowed like a wild bull, and the great god was aroused by the clamour. Enlil heard the clamour and he said to the gods in council, "The uproar of mankind is intolerable and sleep is no longer possibly by reason of the babel." So the gods agreed to exterminate mankind. Enlil did this, but Ea because of his oath warned me in a dream. He whispered their words to my house of reeds, "Reed-house, reed-house! Wall, O Wall, hearken reed-house, wall reflect; O man of Shurrupak, son of Ubara-Tutu; tear down your house and build a boat, abandon possessions and look for life, despise worldly goods and save your soul alive. Tear down your house, I say, and build a boat. These are the measurements of the barque as you shall build her: let her beam equal her length, let her deck be roofed like the vault that covers the abyss; then take up into the boat the seed of all living creatures."

'When I had understood I said to my lord, "Behold, what you have commanded I will honour and perform, but how shall I answer the people, the city, the elders?" Then Ea opened his mouth and said to me, his servant, "Tell them this: I have learnt that Enlil is wrathful against me, I dare no longer walk in his land nor live in his city; I will go down to the Gulf to dwell with Ea my lord. But on you he will rain down abundance, rare fish and shy wild-fowl, a rich harvest-tide. In the evening the rider of the storm will bring you wheat in torrents."

'In the first light of dawn all my household gathered round me, the children brought pitch and the men whatever was necessary. On the fifth day, I laid the keel and the ribs, then I made fast the planking. The ground-space was one acre, each side of the deck measured one hundred and twenty cubits, making a square. I built six decks below, seven in all, I divided them into nine sections with bulkheads between. I drove in wedges where needed, I saw to the punt-poles, and laid in supplies. The carriers brought oil in baskets, I poured pitch into the furnace and asphalt and oil; more oil was consumed in caulking, and more again the master of the boat took into his stores. I slaughtered bullocks for the people and every day I killed sheep. I gave the shipwrights wine to drink as though it were river water, raw wine and red wine and oil and white wine. There was feasting then as there is at the time of the New Year's festival; I myself anointed my head. On the seventh day the boat was complete.

'Then was the launching full of difficulty; there was shifting of the ballast above and below till two thirds was submerged. I loaded into her all that I had of gold and of living things, my family, my kin, the beast of the field both wild and tame, and all the craftsmen. I sent them on board, for the time that Shamash had ordained was already fulfilled when he said, "In the evening, when the rider of the storm sends down the destroying rain, enter the boat and batten her down." The time was fulfilled, the evening came, the rider of the storm sent down the rain. I looked out at the weather and it was terrible, so I too boarded the boat and battened her down. All was now complete, the battening and the caulking; so I handed the tiller to Puzur-Amurri the steersman, with the navigation and the care of the whole boat.

'With the first light of dawn a black cloud came from the horizon; it thundered within where Adad, lord of the storm was riding. In front over hill and plain Shullat and Hanish, heralds of the storm, led on. Then the gods of the abyss rose up;

Nergal pulled out the dams of the nether waters, Ninurta the war-lord threw down the dykes, and the seven judges of hell, the Annunaki, raised their torches, lighting the land with their livid flame. A stupor of despair went up to heaven when the god of the storm turned daylight to darkness, when he smashed the land like a cup. One whole day the tempest raged, gathering fury as it went, it poured over the people like the tides of battle; a man could not see his brother nor the people be seen from heaven. Even the gods were terrified at the flood, they fled to the highest heaven, the firmament of Anu; they crouched against the walls, cowering like curs. Then Ishtar the sweet-voiced Queen of Heaven cried out like a woman in travail: "Alas the days of old are turned to dust because I commanded evil; why did I command this evil in the council of all the gods? I commanded wars to destroy the people, but are they not my people, for I brought them forth? Now like the spawn of fish they float in the ocean." The great gods of heaven and of hell wept, they covered their mouths.

'For six days and six nights the winds blew, torrent and tempest and flood overwhelmed the world, tempest and flood raged together like warring hosts. When the seventh day dawned the storm from the south subsided, the sea grew calm, the flood was stilled; I looked at the face of the world and there was silence, all mankind was turned to clay. The surface of the sea stretched as flat as a roof-top opened a hatch and the light fell on my face. Then I bowed low, I sat down and I wept, the tears streamed down my face, for on every side was the waste of water. I looked for land in vain, but fourteen leagues distant there appeared a mountain, and there the boat grounded; on the mountain of Nisir the boat held fast, she held fast and did not budge. One day she held, and a second day on the mountain of Nisir she held fast and did not budge. A third day, and a fourth day she held fast on the mountain and did not budge; a fifth day and a sixth day she held fast on the mountain. When the seventh day dawned I loosed a dove and let her go. She flew away, but finding no resting-place she returned. Then I loosed a swallow, and she flew away but finding no resting-place she returned. I loosed a raven, she saw that the waters had retreated, she ate, she flew around, she cawed, and she did not come back. Then I threw everything open to the four winds, I made a sacrifice and poured out a libation on the mountain top. Seven and again seven cauldrons I set up on their stands, I heaped up wood and cane and cedar and myrtle. When the gods smelled the sweet savour, they gathered like flies over the sacrifice. Then, at last, Ishtar also came, she lifted her necklace with the jewels of heaven that once Anu had made to please her. "O you gods here present, by the lapis lazuli round my neck I shall remember these days as I remember the jewels of my throat; these last days I shall not forget. Let all the gods gather round the sacrifice, except Enlil. He shall not approach this offering, for without reflection he brought the flood; he consigned my people to destruction."

'When Enlil had come, when he saw the boat, he was wrath and swelled with anger at the gods, the host of heaven, "Has any of these mortals escaped? Not one was to have survived the destruction." Then the god of the wells and canals Ninurta opened his mouth and said to the warrior Enlil, "Who is there of the gods that can devise without Ea? It is Ea alone who knows all things." Then Ea opened his mouth and spoke to warrior Enlil, "Wisest of gods, hero Enlil, how could you so senselessly bring down the flood?

*Lay upon the sinner his sin,*
*Lay upon the transgressor his transgression,*
*Punish him a little when he breaks loose,*
*Do not drive him too hard or he perishes;*
*Would that a lion had ravaged mankind*

*Rather than the flood,*
*Would that a wolf had ravaged mankind*
*Rather than the flood,*
*Would that famine had wasted the world*
*Rather than the flood,*
*Would that pestilence had wasted mankind*
*Rather than the flood.*

'It was not I that revealed the secret of the gods; the wise man learned it in a dream. Now take your counsel what shall be done with him."

'Then Enlil went up into the boat, he took me by the hand and my wife and made us enter the boat and kneel down on either side, he standing between us. He touched our foreheads to bless us saying, "In time past Utnapishtim was a mortal man; henceforth he and his wife shall live in the distance at the mouth of the rivers." Thus it was that the gods took me and placed me here to live in the distance, at the mouth of the rivers."

Compare this story with Noah's flood story below, written around 562 BCE—at least two thousand years later than the version in The Epic of Gilgamesh:

GENESIS 6

1 Now it came to pass, when men came to multiply on the face of the earth, and daughters were born to them,

2 that the sons of God saw the daughters of men, that they were beautiful; and they took wives for themselves of all whom they chose.

3 And the Lord said, "My spirit shall not strive with man forever, for he is indeed flesh; yet his days shall be one hundred and twenty years."

4 There were giants on earth in those days, and also afterward,

when the sons of God came in to the daughters of men and they bore children to them. Those were the mighty men, who were of old, men of renown.

5 Then the Lord saw that the wickedness of man was great in the earth, and that every intent of the thoughts of his heart was only evil continually.

6 And the Lord was sorry that He made man on the earth, and He was grieved in His heart.

7 So the Lord said, "I will destroy man whom I have created from the face of the earth, both man and beast, creeping thing and birds of the air, for I am sorry that I have made them."

8 But Noah found grace in the eyes of the Lord.

9 This is the genealogy of Noah. Noah was a just man, perfect in his generations. Noah walked with God.

10 And Noah begot three sons: Shem, Ham, and Japheth.

11 The earth was also corrupt before God, and the earth was filled with violence.

12 So God looked upon the earth, and indeed it was corrupt; for all flesh had corrupted their way on the earth.

13 And God said to Noah, "The end of all flesh has come before Me, for the earth is filled with violence through them; and behold, I will destroy them with the earth.

14 "Make yourself an ark of gopherwood; make rooms in the ark, and cover it inside and outside with pitch.

15 "And this is how you shall make it: The length of the ark shall be three hundred cubits, its width fifty cubits, and its height thirty cubits.

16 "You shall make a window for the ark, and you shall finish it to a cubit from above; and set the door of the ark in its side. You shall make it with lower, second and third decks.

17 "And behold I myself am bringing floodwaters upon the earth, to destroy from under heaven all flesh in which is the breath of life; everything that is on the earth shall die.

18 "But I will establish My covenant with you; and you shall go into the ark—you, your sons, your wife, and your sons' wives with you.

19 "And of every living thing of all flesh you shall bring two of every sort into the ark, to keep them alive with you; they shall be male and female.

20 "Of the birds after their kind, of animals after their kind, and of every creeping thing of the earth after its kind, two of every kind will come to you to keep them alive.

21 "And you shall take for yourself of all food that is eaten, and you shall gather it to yourself; and it shall be food for you and for them."

22 Thus Noah did; according to all that God commanded him, so he did.

## GENESIS 7

1 Then the Lord said to Noah, "Come into the ark, you and all your household, because I have seen that you are righteous before Me in this generation.

2 "You shall take with you seven each of every clean animal, a male and his female; two each of animals that are unclean, a male and his female;

3 "also seven each of birds of the air, male and female, to keep the species alive on the face of all the earth.

4 "For after seven more days I will cause it to rain on the earth forty days and forty nights, and I will destroy from the face of the earth all living things that I have made."

5 And Noah did according to all that the Lord commanded him.

6 Noah was six hundred years old when the floodwaters were on the earth.

7 So Noah, with his sons, his wife, and his sons' wives, went into the ark because of the waters of the flood.

8 Of clean animals, of animals that are unclean, of birds, and of everything that creeps on the earth,

9 two by two they went into the ark to Noah, male and female, as God had commanded Noah.

10 And it came to pass after seven days that the waters of the flood were on the earth.

11 In the six hundredth year of Noah's life, in the second month, the seventeenth day of the month, on that day all the fountains of the great deep were broken up, and the windows of heaven were opened.

12 And the rain was on the earth forty days and forty nights.

13 On the very same day Noah and Noah's sons, Shem, Ham and Japheth, and Noah's wife and the three wives of his sons with them, entered the ark—

14 they and every beast after its kind, all cattle after their kind, every creeping thing that creeps on the earth after its kind, and every bird after its kind, every bird of every sort.

15 And they went into the ark to Noah, two by two, of all flesh in which is the breath of life.

16 So those that entered, male and female of all flesh, went in as God had commanded him; and the Lord shut him in.

17 Now the flood was on the earth forty days. The waters increased and lifted up the ark, and it rose high above the earth.

18 The waters prevailed and greatly increased on the earth, and the ark moved about on the surface of the waters.

19 And the waters prevailed exceedingly on the earth, and all the high hills under the whole heaven were covered.

20 The waters prevailed fifteen cubits upward, and the mountains were covered.

21 And all flesh died that moved on the earth: birds and cattle and beasts and every creeping thing that creeps on the earth, and every man.

22 All in whose nostrils was the breath of the spirit of life, all that was on the dry land, died.

23 So He destroyed all living things which were on the face of the ground: both man and cattle, creeping thing and bird of the air. They were destroyed from the earth. Only Noah and those who were with him in the ark remained alive.

24 And the waters prevailed on the earth one hundred and fifty days.

## GENESIS 8

1 Then God remembered Noah, and every living thing, and all the animals that were with him in the ark. And God made a wind to pass over the earth, and the waters subsided.

2 The fountains of the deep and the windows of the heaven were also stopped, and the rain from heaven was restrained.

3 And the waters receded continually from the earth. At the end of the hundred and fifty days the waters decreased.

4 Then the ark rested in the seventh month, the seventeenth day of the month, on the mountains of Ararat.

5 And the waters decreased continually until the tenth month. In the tenth month, on the first day of the month, the tops of the mountains were seen.

6 So it came to pass, at the end of forty days, that Noah opened the window of the ark which he had made.

7 Then he sent out a raven, which kept going to and fro until the waters had dried up from the earth.

8 He also sent out from himself a dove, to see if the waters had receded from the face of the ground.

9 But the dove found no resting place for the sole of her foot, and she returned into the ark to him, for the waters were on the face of the whole earth. So he put out his hand and took her, and drew her into the ark to himself.

10 And he waited yet another seven days, and again he sent the dove out from the ark.

11 Then the dove came to him in the evening, and behold, a freshly plucked olive leaf was in her mouth; and Noah knew that the waters had receded from the earth.

12 So he waited yet another seven days and sent out the dove, which did not return again to him anymore.

13 And it came to pass in the six hundred and first year, in the first month, the first day of the month, that the waters were dried up from the earth; and Noah removed the covering of the ark and looked, and indeed the surface of the ground was dry.

14 And in the second month, on the twenty-seventh day of the month, the earth was dried.

15 Then God spoke to Noah, saying,

16 "Go out of the ark, you and your wife, and your sons and your sons' wives with you.

17 "Bring out with you every living thing of all flesh that is with you: birds and cattle and every creeping thing that creeps

on the earth, so that they may abound on the earth, and be fruitful and multiply on the earth."

18 So Noah went out, and his sons and his wife and his sons' wives with him.

19 Every animal, every creeping thing, every bird, and whatever creeps on the earth, according to their families, went out of the ark ...

Be reminded the Mesopotamian text from The Epic of Gilgamesh was written in cuneiform long before the Phoenician alphabet came into use, and longer still before the Hebrew alphabet that was derived from it. Had any professor of literature, or even an English high-school teacher, compared the story of Noah with the previously quoted Mesopotamian text, I do not believe the student submitting Noah's story would have received a passing grade—most likely a big, fat F for his or her obvious reliance on another's text, despite the few changes and additions. But this isn't college or high school. It's the Bible, and its similarity here to a much older text is worthy of pause. Intertextuality raises important questions regarding the very foundation upon which rests a reverence for the Bible as a flawless, sacred work handed down from above—or, in this case, shot down from above.

Is it really a concern? The small portion of Genesis illustrated above—three chapters out of sixty, or 5 percent—obviously came from an outside source. When added alongside the ten biblical books that follow through to Kings II, this indiscretion may deserve only an asterisk. Nonetheless, it does give one pause. (Biblical scholars widely accept that the book of Ruth was inserted between Judges and Samuel I long after Genesis–Kings II was composed, for reasons not exactly known but fun to hypothesize—I invite all of you to take a shot at it.)

It is critical to note one important change between the two texts: the cause of the flood. In The Epic, the important god Enlil brought about the flood because the people were so loud and noisy that it interrupted his sleep. If ever one tried to get a good night's sleep in an older hotel in Manhattan, he or she could readily relate to Enlil's frustration and anger. In Genesis, the Lord caused the "unnatural" flooding because of the "wickedness" of the people. This provides at least a good peek into the mind(s) of those or the one who authored the biblical story of Noah. Before giving up a large quantity of time considering this interesting change to the story, a second biblical intertextual case must be described.

## CHAPTER 4

# Intertextuality, Case Two

## DAVID VERSUS GOLIATH AND THE EPIC OF GILGAMESH

The intertextuality observed in the previous chapter clearly illustrates the use of an extra-biblical Sumerian literary source, the much earlier Epic of Gilgamesh. The biblical text of Noah and the flood told a similar story as that found in The Epic, but changed the cause of the flood.

In this next example of intertextuality, you'll see several crucial changes made to the story of a duel between the Epic's hero, Gilgamesh, and the monster Humbaba, in order to produce the popular story of David and Goliath. The many changes effectively camouflaged the use of The Epic, all of which were in keeping with the Hebrew notion of an ideal model king befitting of their society. The David and Goliath story was craftily reconstructed but clearly inspired by The Epic of Gilgamesh.

Most historians agree a man with the name Gilgamesh ruled as king of Urek (biblical: Erech) sometime during the twenty-seventh century BCE. In later years, Gilgamesh came to be remarkably glorified, first in Sumerian literature and later in most other Near East languages as well, making him the most celebrated, the most admired, and the most familiar epic hero of the ancient Near East. Sometime around 1700 BCE, the exaggerated exploits of Gilgamesh related in tales and poems were collected by a Babylonian or two and compiled into a single epic, The Epic of Gilgamesh. It was a hit—a big hit.

Among the many readers of The Epic were the Hebrews, as you have already seen. Thanks to the discovery of The Epic's clay tablets, we have been provided with illuminating insights into the development of important parts of the Hebrew Bible. The historian P. Kyle McCarter also drew parallels between the biblical story of Jacob and Esau and The Epic's important thematic conflict between civilization and nature, man versus beast. Are these the only instances of intertextuality? No, they are not! There's much more Epic in the Bible than Noah and the flood and Esau and Jacob. The Epic exerted a profoundly significant influence upon the development of the Bible that extends beyond all that has been written on the topic to date.

The biblical story of David and Goliath is very popular. A comparison of this story with The Epic's prologue, second chapter ("The Forest Journey"), third chapter ("Ishtar and Gilgamesh, and the Death of Enkidu"), and seventh chapter ("The Death of Gilgamesh") will yield the important revelation that this popular biblical story was not only inspired by The Epic, but conceived and written to fit within The Epic's framework.

Two very obvious similarities connect the two stories, but what's more interesting is how the biblical writers of the David story adjusted The Epic text to express different religious ideas—concepts that suited their own spirituality. While much of the Noah story was taken nearly verbatim from The

Epic, here we find the use of contrast with The Epic woven into the David story, clearly for the purpose of differentiating Hebrew intellectual and religious thought from that of the Mesopotamians.

The Epic of Gilgamesh and the Biblical Story of David

First, let's compare the two stories' heroes: David, the king of the Israelites, and Gilgamesh, the king of Uruk.

The Epic begins with a short, three-paragraph prologue describing the mental and physical attributes of Gilgamesh. It begins with a boom: "I will proclaim to the world the deeds of Gilgamesh. This was the man to whom all things were known; this was the king who knew the countries of the world. … When the gods created Gilgamesh, they gave him a perfect body." The Epic credits Shamash, the sun god, as the one who endowed Gilgamesh with beauty, and the god of the storm, Adad, for endowing him with courage: "his beauty perfect … terrifying like a great wild bull. Two thirds they made him god and one third they made him man." It concludes with a description of all the great things Gilgamesh built in Urek. In the minds of the Mesopotamians, Gilgamesh had all the attributes fit for a king, as a builder who also possessed general knowledge of other peoples and their countries, strength, courage, physical beauty, and divinity (as Gilgamesh was two-thirds god).

But in the minds of the ancient Hebrews, a great, effective king may possess attributes unlike those of Gilgamesh, and here we find an important (and intended) contrast with The Epic. An important contrast can be easily noted in 1 Samuel 10:23–24, after Samuel was instructed by the Lord to seek out a king for His people. In these verses, Samuel's emphasis on the height of Saul was duly noted. Saul stood "taller than any of the people from his shoulders upward," a physical reference reminiscent of Gilgamesh. Samuel was later reminded by the Lord that tallness alone doesn't make a king.

Compare the description of Gilgamesh's attributes with a description of David, a different sort from the Mesopotamian king. 1 Samuel 16 begins the search for a new king following the tall man Saul's fall from grace with the Lord. Samuel again looks first at Eliab and declares that "Surely the Lord's anointed is before him" (16:6). In 16:7, the Lord advises Samuel to "not look at his appearance or at his physical stature, because I have refused him. For the Lord does not see as man sees; for man looks at the outward appearance, but the Lord looks at the heart." This is a very important contrast with The Epic's royal attribute of a "perfect body." The Hebrew Lord looks *inside* the man to find strength and perfection in his heart and in his soul, rather than looking at the outside of a man for "beauty perfect," muscles, height, or any other specific outer trait.

The biblical story goes on to describe how the Lord rejects the next nine would-be kings before deciding upon David. In 1 Samuel 16:11, David enters the picture. When asked by Samuel if "all the young men are here," Jesse replies, "Their remains yet the youngest, and there he is, keeping the sheep."

The comparison of David, the youngest son, perhaps no more than a boy, "keeping sheep" with Gilgamesh, who is two-thirds god and one-third "perfect" man, is one of stark contrast. Think of what Hebrew thought implies with these strikingly different attributes. You don't have to be two-thirds god and one-third man of perfect body to slay a giant and become a king. Inner strength and spirit alone—attributes within reach of all of us, including young boys keeping sheep—can make one a slayer of giants. This idea has a lot of appeal among common man, and is very inspiring.

On the other hand, courage (and the expectations of glory that come with courageous acts) is an important attribute fit for the Hebrew hero, as it was for Gilgamesh. Here we see obvious connecting similarities between the two stories. Compare how the stories' heroes respond to the proposition of a fight with each of their gigantic and ferocious opposing foes, and their expectations of glory if victorious.

"Gilgamesh," Enkidu begins in a pointed warning, "the watchmen of the forest never sleeps." Gilgamesh replies, "How is this, already you are afraid! … Forward, there is nothing to fear!" Gilgamesh receives more cautionary counsel from Enkidu: "Why do you crave to do this thing, Gilgamesh? It is not an equal struggle when one fights with Humbaba; he is a great warrior, a battering ram. … We have heard that Humbaba is not like men who die, his weapons are such that none can stand against them …" Gilgamesh replies, "How shall I answer them: shall I say I am afraid of Humbaba, I will sit at home all the rest of my days? … I will go to the country where the cedar is cut. I will set up my name where the names of famous men are written; and where no man's name is written I will raise a monument to the gods." Expectations of great glory and enrichment are motivations possessed by Gilgamesh, should he be victorious in his fight with the giant, Humbaba.

Compare this dialogue with 1 Samuel 17:24–26, 32, and 33: "all the men of Israel, when they saw the man [Goliath] fled from him and were dreadfully afraid." David, like Gilgamesh, responds with courage: "Let no man's heart fail because of him; your servant will go and fight with the Philistine." David is also warned, as was Gilgamesh: "You are not able to go against this Philistine to fight with him; for you are a youth, and he a man of war from his youth." Not persuaded, the courageous David proceeds with his fight against his gigantic foe, Goliath, and like Gilgamesh, David expects glory and enrichment to follow, should he prevail over the giant: "David spoke to the men who stood by him saying, 'What shall be done for the man who kills him? For who is this uncircumcised Philistine that he should defy the armies of the Living God?'" And the men of Israel say, "… and it shall be the man who kills him the king will enrich with great riches, will give him his daughter, and give his father's house exemption from taxes in Israel." Great glory and enrichment will come to David if he is victorious.

Similarities connecting the two stories are also quite obvious when we compare the stories' villains, Goliath and Humbaba. They are both giants casting fear to any who come near, and holding seemingly overwhelming odds against any challenger. Humbaba, Gilgamesh's foe, resides in the "uncivilized" forest,

for in the forest lives Humbaba whose name is "Hugeness," "a ferocious giant." … When he roars it is like the torrent of a storm … What man would willingly walk into that country and explore its depths? I tell you, weakness overpowers whoever goes near it: it is no equal struggle when one fights with Humbaba, that battering-ram.

In no uncertain terms, the stage is set for an epic struggle between good and evil, between hero and villain, between Gilgamesh and Humbaba.

In 1 Samuel we read of another seemingly unequal struggle between good and evil, between a courageous hero and a villain of gigantic proportion. Goliath is a giant standing "six cubits and a span … a champion from the camp of the Philistines." He hurls insults at his lowly adversaries, the Israelites, and taunts those who dare fight the powerful Philistines: "Why have you come out to line up for battle? Am I not a Philistine, and you the servants of Saul?" This compares with the quote above from The Epic: "What man would willingly walk into that country and explore its depths?"

In both the Mesopotamian and Hebrew societies, we find that when one is courageous enough to face overwhelming odds in battle with an evil giant and prevails, he shall be anointed with heroic status, great glory, and royalty.

The settings of the stories are also similar in notable ways. In The Epic we read, "Because of the evil that is in the land, we will go to the forest and destroy the evil ..." Because of the evil (the Philistines) in the land of Israel, the Israelites will go to the Valley of Elah and destroy the evil. Both stories used real locations for their settings. The Valley of Elah is a real place. The forest, the land of cedars described in The Epic, is also a real location.

Another important and interesting point of comparison is the weapon fitted upon each warrior. Gilgamesh is fitted with "axes of nine score pounds ... great swords they cast with blades of six score pounds each, with pommels and hilts of thirty pounds ... the axe 'Might of Heroes' and the bow of Anshan ..." Later, Gilgamesh strapped on his breastplate, which weighed thirty shekels. (The giant Goliath's "coat of mail" weighed five thousand shekels.)

In 1 Samuel 17:38 and 39, we read, "So Saul clothed David with his armor, and he put a bronze helmet on his head; he also clothed him with a coat of mail ... David fastened his sword to his armor and tried to walk ..."

But here, when it comes to the use of these weapons, we see another very important and purposeful contrast between the two stories. In 1 Samuel 17:39, after the young David's troubled attempt to walk, David says, "I cannot walk with these" and takes them off. It is interesting to note that the weapons used by Gilgamesh to confront his giant foe are very similar to those rejected by David. Afterward, as many know, David set out to select "five smooth stones from the brook" and arms himself with only a sling.

By rejecting weapons similar to those of Gilgamesh and taking only a simple sling into a battle with a giant foe, David illustrates a fundamental principle of Hebrew religious belief that the true source of power and strength is the Lord. This is best explained by the dialogue between David and Goliath in 1 Samuel 17, when Goliath mocks David by saying, "Am I a dog that you come to me with sticks?" And David replies, "You come to me with a sword, with a spear, with a javelin. But I come to you in the name of the Lord … know that there is a God in Israel." In other words, if the Lord resides within your land and within your soul, and you are in His service, you can overcome an opposing fearsome giant armed to the teeth—and triumph using only a simple sling. From the Lord you receive true strength, not from your weapons.

Although it's easy to see contrast between the above dialogue and The Epic, it's important to point out that in The Epic, we also read how Gilgamesh received support from a god, Shamash—but in vastly different form. When we read that Humbaba "came from his strong house of cedar" and "fastened his eye, the eye of death" upon Gilgamesh, we find, surprisingly, a frightened Gilgamesh. Gilgamesh "called to Shamash and his tears were flowing, 'O glorious Shamash, I have followed the road you commanded but now if you send no succore how shall I escape? … Glorious Shamash heard his prayer and summoned the great wind," a wind that literally blew Humbaba away, rendering him "unable to go forward or back." Gilgamesh, grateful for Shamash's aid, shouts, "By the life of Ninsun my mother and divine Lugulbanda my father, in the Country of the Living, in this land I have discovered your dwelling." With that help from Shamash, Gilgamesh goes on to defeat Humbaba.

This is followed by a very interesting quote of great importance. Gilgamesh adds, "my weak arms and my small weapons I have brought to this Land against you, and now I will enter your house." The phrases "weak arms" and "small weapons" are very reminiscent of David's sling and stone. This simple quote in The Epic alludes to the idea that weak arms and small weapons, when given the aid of a god, can level the playing field between man and giant—clearly a theme found in David and Goliath as well. But the biblical contrast between Gilgamesh's weapons and David's sling seems emphasized, and intended to reinforce this concept beyond the brief allusion to it in The Epic.

David and Goliath's connection to The Epic is further supported by the stories' telling of the deaths of the two villainous giants. In The Epic we read, "[Gilgamesh] took the axe in his hand, he drew the sword from his belt, and he struck Humbaba with a thrust of the sword to the neck," and after two additional blows, Humbaba falls. In only one verse, 1 Samuel 17:49, David swiftly kills Goliath with a stone to the forehead, and in the following verse, 1 Samuel 17:50, we read, "So David prevailed over the Philistine ... But was no sword in David's hand." It's hard not to see the parallel here with The Epic. The emphasis on the fact that David had no sword (only the Lord in his heart) seems clearly intended as a pointed contrast with The Epic. (Please note, however, that David used Goliath's sword to sever his head.)

There are also interesting parallels between the presentations of the severed heads of the villains; David and Gilgamesh each came before their respective overseers, Saul and the Mesopotamian god Enlil, and Saul and Enlil responded differently.

In the Epic we read, "they kissed the ground and dropped the shroud and set the head before [Enlil]. But Enlil was angered. 'Why did you do this thing? From henceforth may the fire be on your faces, may it eat the bread you eat, may it drink where you drink.'"

In 1 Samuel 17: 54 and 57, we read, "And David took the head of the Philistine and brought it to Jerusalem ... Abner took [David] and brought him before Saul with the head of the Philistine in his hand." In 1 Samuel 18:6–9 we read, "… the women had come out of all cities of Israel, singing and dancing … Saul has slain his thousands, And David his ten thousands. Then Saul was very angry, and the saying displeased him. … So Saul eyed David from that day forward."

While Saul is clearly threatened by the rising star of David, Enlil is enraged by Gilgamesh's hand in the death of his beloved creation, Humbaba.

From here, the David story seemingly continues along its own path until the story nears its end with David's impending death. Here again we see important parallels with The Epic following the death of Enkidu. In 2 Samuel 22, we come to David's song of deliverance as he "spoke to the Lord the words of this song." It's a song of some length—fifty verses. The words of this song describe David's love of the Lord who was his "sword"—the constant, benevolent companion residing in his heart through thick and thin. Compare the poetry of this song with the poetic words of Gilgamesh following the death of Enkidu, his friend and foil, his constant and benevolent companion through thick and thin. The relationship between Gilgamesh and Enkidu closely resembles David's relationship with the Lord. David says,

The Lord is my rock and my fortress and my deliverer.
The God of my strength, in whom I will trust;
My shield and the horn of my salvation
My stronghold and my refuge;

Gilgamesh says,

O Enkidu, my brother,
You were the axe at my side
My hand's strength, the sword in my belt,
The shield before me,

A glorious robe, my fairest ornament;

Both songs seem to share the same poetry, the same rhythm. Both songs express the same theme, the same love and devotion to a most revered companion. Both songs reminisce. Yet the contrast between the Lord and Enkidu is also easy to see. In the mind of the Hebrews, the Lord is the only god. In David's song, we read,

For who is God, except the Lord?

And who is rock, except our God?

… *He* is the tower of salvation to His king

And shows mercy to his anointed,

To David and his descendants forever more.

On the other hand, Enkidu is much harder to define. "You are wise, Enkidu, and now you have become 'like a god.'" In the introduction to The Epic by N. K. Sanders, we also read that Enkidu was molded out of clay by Aruru, goddess of creation, "'in the image and of the essence of Anu' the sky god and *Ninurta* the war god … he is 'wild or natural man'; he was later considered a patron god of animals and may have been the hero of another cycle." Enkidu's power and accessibility was not like that of the Lord's, and his immortality was, at best, cyclical.

In contrast to Gilgamesh's Enkidu, David's companion, the Lord, is well defined, absent of all ambiguity. He is The Lord, is God, is immortal; he is not simply "like a god." Although the relationship between David and the Lord is very similar to the relationship between Gilgamesh and Enkidu, the Hebrew Lord and the somewhat animal-like Enkidu are two very different entities. We must also be mindful of what we read in Genesis: the Lord created man in "His likeness" and gave man "dominion" over all animals.

Then we come to the death of both of our heroes, and parallels between the two stories emerge one last time. The main story line of The Epic seem to ask, *Is Gilgamesh going to enjoy everlasting life as do the gods?* He was not so destined, and was denied everlasting life. "The king has laid himself down and will not rise again, The Lord of Kullab will not rise again; … He is gone into the mountain, he will not come again; … On the bed of fate he lies, he will not rise again …" Why, one may ask, was Gilgamesh denied everlasting life? Apparently, being "like a god" doesn't mean he is a god. As great a man as Gilgamesh was, his greatness was counted on an earthly scale, whereas the gods are from somewhere above. There is man and there are the gods, and that's how it was.

As for David's "bed of fate," in 1 Kings 2 we read, "now the days of David drew near," and he said to his son Solomon, "I go the way of all the earth; be strong, therefore, and prove yourself a man," and later we read, "So David rested with his fathers, and was buried in the City of David." Like Gilgamesh, David went "the way of all the earth" and was laid to rest in his grave.

Such parallels clearly indicate a connection between the two stories.

It is interesting to contemplate the considerable amount of text missing from The Epic of Gilgamesh. The Bible may provide clues as to the contents of that text. In chapter 2 of The Epic, "The Forest Journey," we read of how Enlil raged at Gilgamesh following his slaughter of Humbaba: "From henceforth may the fire be on your faces, may it eat the bread you eat, may it drink where you drink." However, chapter 7, "The Death of Gilgamesh," begins, "The destiny was fulfilled which the father of the gods, Enlil of the mountain, had decreed for Gilgamesh … none will leave a monument for generations to come to compare with his." One may reasonably speculate that somewhere in the missing text of The Epic was a similar reconciliation between Enlil and Gilgamesh. If so, the accommodation between Saul and David that we read of in 1 Samuel may have been influenced by this, even if it remained more uneasy than that described in The Epic. Although such speculations are interesting to consider, short of our archaeologists someday uncovering the remaining missing texts from the Epic, it appears we are limited to only speculation.

## CHAPTER 5

# In the Course of Human Events:

## (THE HISTORY OF EGYPT, BABYLON, AND JERUSALEM IN THE SIXTH CENTURY BCE)

The role of outside sources in the writing of the Bible is interesting, but the Bible's composition is far more accurately and much more comprehensively explained by history, especially the important historical events that took place a few decades before and during the time that the first books of the Bible, Genesis through Kings II, were composed.

As stated earlier, had it not been for these events, the Bible as we know it would never have been written. Although many cling to various beliefs regarding the Bible, ranging from the totality of its literal truth as the word of God handed down by the Lord Himself (orthodox doctrine) to various "conservative" and more liberal "reforming" modifications of interpretation, most of these beliefs and interpretations simply fail to really explain the Bible. As hard it may be for many to accept, the Bible is a product of men sitting down to write a book for a specific audience to effect a specific result brought about purely by geography, competing powers, and a series of interconnecting events.

As our knowledge of ancient Near East history has grown from the ever-increasing number of archaeological samples, the improved techniques for dating, the accumulation of data, and the increased collaboration and improved research methodologies among departments of history and archaeology at universities throughout the world, this knowledge has enabled our researchers and professors to more accurately date the biblical books' original compositions.

Many biblical historians have suggested composition dates over the years, and a common consensus has formed that narrows these dates down more precisely. Among such historians is Professor Serge Frolov of Southern Methodist University, a leading member of the University's Department of Religion whose courses focus on the Hebrew Bible and the books found in the Old Testament. Thanks to his diligent research and careful analysis, Dr. Frolov has precisely dated Genesis–Kings II.

My research forming the foundation of this book lends strong support to Dr. Frolov's dating. I began to collaborate with Dr. Frolov in the winter of 2009 after composing a paper connecting the David and Goliath story with The Epic of Gilgamesh (text that now appears in Part One of this book). Based on Dr. Frolov's excellent research, Genesis through Kings II was written in or near Babylon by a group of exiled Jews from 562 to 560 BCE following the death of Babylon's famous king, Nebuchadnezzar.

Simply winding the clock back a few decades before this momentous event took place and recounting the historical events that occurred in the ancient Near East during this time, and then standing those events side by side comparatively with the Bible, will clearly and precisely explain why the project was undertaken, why the biblical story took the shape it did, and who specifically it was written for. The narrow but noble goal for which these ten books were intended was simply to hold the writers' community together during this most severe time in their history. Indeed, the writers' efforts were also heroic. Little did they know how much their project would alter the course of history and shape our future Western societies, institutions, and cultural experience.

Together, let's take a journey back to the time and place the Bible was written: the sixth century BCE, along the southwest shore of the Mediterranean Sea, where a resurgent Egypt was bouncing back from decades of decline. To the east also sat Babylonia, a once-great ancient civilization that had declined but was grandly resurging once more. Between these two magnificent but also competing ancient civilizations sat a comparatively young and seemingly insignificant peaceful people, the ancient Hebrews, who had first begun settling in and around Jerusalem and Judea around 1250 BCE or possibly a few decades later. The shores along the southwestern Mediterranean and overland trade roads facilitated travel, interaction, and economy among the peoples of these locations.

The Bible would not have come into existence without these geographic and historical circumstances, nor without the convergence of a series of unpredictable historical events that had taken place during the years just preceding the biblical project. Ultimately, human resolve in the face of severe adversity is what brought forth the Bible's creation.

The first dominoes that put in motion this series of successive events were tipped by the hand of Egypt.

A favored and highly respected book published in 1998, *The Ancient Near East* by William E. Dustan of North Carolina University, is an excellent and very reliable historical survey of its title's namesake, the ancient Near East. According to Dunstan's considered survey, nearly two thousand years after the great pyramids were built, following a static five-hundred-year period of eclipse in Egyptian history that began around 1100 BCE, Egypt began to emerge once again, as described earlier. In an era known as the Saite Revival, the Twenty-Sixth Dynasty founded by the Egyptian king Psamtik I (664–610 BCE) ushered in a period of "remarkable Egyptian splendor" that would last through 525 BCE—nearly 140 years. Psamtik's son, Necho II (610–595 BCE) followed his father's long and glorious reign. Despite lasting only fifteen years, Necho II's reign was one of unimaginable consequence. The king was ambitious. He was the first to initiate the construction of a canal connecting the Nile to the Red Sea, an endeavor that was eventually abandoned. Despite the outcome, this grand effort illuminates Necho II's will and determination to substantially increase trade with Arabia by increasing shipping along the coasts of the Mediterranean, and illustrates how determined and confident Necho II really was. Even the famous Greek historian, Herodotus, recognized Necho II's achievements.

But ambition and confidence have consequences—sometimes unintended consequences. One such unintended consequence of great importance came about after Necho II chose to support the ultimately losing side between two warring parties, the waning Assyrians rather than the upstart Neo-Babylonians. The balance of power in the west had already began migrating away from the Assyrians, who had earlier wrestled it away from the Nubian and Libyan kings occupying Egypt, but was now beginning to revert back to the Egyptians again. Mindful of Egypt's onetime Assyrian benefactors, Necho II supported Assyria in their fight against the Neo-Babylonians who settled in and around Babylon. Known also as the Chaldeans, the Neo-Babylonians had adopted Babylonian customs and culture.

The great and long-reigning Chaldean king, Nebuchadnezzar II (605–562 BCE) was a symbol of Chaldean prosperity. Determined to restore Babylon to its ancient splendor, Nebuchadnezzar succeeded in turning the city into one of grand opulence. Although the revered and beautiful Hanging Gardens of Babylon were later proclaimed to be a wonder of the world, it was the famous forty-foot-tall Ishtar Gate, dedicated to the goddess of sexual love and war, that was the most fitting symbol of Nebuchadnezzar II. The Chaldean king proved a formidable match for Egypt's leader, Necho II, and the forces sent to support the Assyrians were subsequently nullified.

After the Assyrian defeat at Carchemish at the hands of the Chaldeans, the Egyptians were forced to withdraw from the west. Ultimately, the defeat of Necho's Egyptian forces in this battle produced a string of events with consequences upon human history arguably greater than any outcome from any other battle in human history to date. This stirring up of Nebuchadnezzar II's wrath directly instigated a series of occurrences leading directly to the Bible's creation, an event that ultimately made the Egyptian and Babylonian historic consequence pale in comparison.

Following their victory at Carchemish, the Babylonians (or Chaldeans) became the undisputed power in the west. Nonetheless, Necho's Egypt remained the predominant power in the east. The king of Egypt, perhaps personally embarrassed and haunted by the loss at Carchemish, continued to cause trouble by inciting hostile sentiment toward Babylon among some of the peoples occupying his realm. One was a seemingly inconsequential group, the Hebrews—also known as Judeans, Israelites, or Jews. Soon after, the Hebrews became embroiled in a plot contrived by Egypt to demonstrate hostility toward Babylon that became so provocative that Nebuchadnezzar marched his armies some five hundred miles to invade and conquer Judea.

In 597 BCE, the Babylonians entered Jerusalem, destroyed the temple, carted off much of the Hebrews' treasure, and purportedly replaced the eighteen-year-old Hebrew king, Jehoiachin, with his uncle, Zedekiah, who then ruled over Jerusalem as a Babylonian-controlled puppet. Then, less than ten years later, in 588 BCE, Egyptian influence somehow prompted Zedekiah, who most likely wanted to expel Babylonian influence from Jerusalem, into yet another hapless rebellion against Babylonia that provoked a much more severe Babylonian retribution. After laying siege to Jerusalem in late 588 BCE, the Babylonians breached the city's walls less than two years later, and Jerusalem once again fell into the hands of Nebuchadnezzar—only this time, the consequences were far worse than they had been in 597 BCE.

Already thumped hard by the nearly two-year Babylonian economic blockade, Jerusalem was put down on its heels once again, suffering unimaginable hardship--and it didn't end there. Nebuchadnezzar forces carried off everything of value found in the city and then separated the noblemen, leaders, and all members of the economic upper class from their remaining Hebrew brethren. Every one of those elite citizens was marched off to exile in Babylon, leaving their far less fortunate Hebrew brethren in unimaginable economic squalor and social disarray.

Sever the head from the body, and the body dies, right? The Babylonians certainly presumed that the Hebrew population remaining in Judah would wither away, fading from history and into oblivion. Undoubtedly, the leaderless lower classes of Judeans left behind in Jerusalem faced insurmountable circumstances, to say the least. To say the more, in 586 BCE, the Hebrew people appeared to begin their march into extinction.

## CHAPTER 6

# The Writing of the Bible

There remains still another very important historical and haunting event that occurred well over a hundred years before the events leading to the exile in 586 BCE. Like those already described, this event directly influenced the mind-set of the biblical writers that came to be. This event is the curious case of the Northern Kingdom, Israel.

Historians mark the end of the kingdom at 722 BCE, 160 years before the biblical writers sat down to their work. A few years prior to 722 BCE, Israel suffered a devastating defeat by Assyria under the rule of Tiglath-Pileser III. Not long after, the leader of what remained of Israel, Hoshea, led a fruitless rebellion against Assyria that quickly proved to be as fatal a debacle as it would the following time for Zedekiah 136 years later in 586 BCE. Interestingly, following their drubbing of the Hebrews, Assyria annexed the territory and exiled thousands of Hebrew members of the upper classes to northern Mesopotamia, leaving the remaining Hebrew masses to melt away. These remaining Hebrews later came to be remembered as "the lost tribes of Israel."

The events leading up to their demise are eerily similar to those that had befallen the Southern Kingdom in 586 BCE. With lingering memory of the "lost tribes" of the north haunting their hearts and minds, many of those exiled to Babylonia certainly feared the same fate would befall their fellow sisters and brethren left behind in the sacked and defeated city of Jerusalem and the surrounding areas composing the Southern Kingdom of Judea. But what could they possibly do? What weapons did the exiles have? What power did they possess that could turn the high tides of adversity, poverty, and destruction sweeping over their leaderless people while they were exiled in a far-off land? Their people's situation in Jerusalem must have seemed hopeless, but the biblical writers were determined to do what they could. They wrote the Bible's all-important first books.

Eventually, the months following the exile in 586 BCE turned into years, and the years into decades. Although haunted by thoughts of those left behind dwelling in squalor, despair, and hopelessness, the Jews exiled in Babylonia fared well. They were permitted to pursue their lives in one of the most beautiful cities in the ancient Near East, Babylon—home of the Hanging Gardens, the Ishtar Gate, and all the opulence of Nebuchadnezzar's construction, including his famous palace and ziggurat, or Etemenanki, more popularly known as the Tower of Babel. The Hebrew exiles were afforded many personal freedoms, including the pursuit of commercial endeavors, farming, and other means of self-support. It's easy to imagine why, by all recorded accounts, the vast majority of exiles chose to remain in Babylon after Cyrus the Great granted them their freedom to return to Judea in 537 BCE, just two years after he conquered the city. Who wouldn't remain in Babylon, an opulent city of beauty and abundance, especially among those still alive after nearly fifty years in Babylon?

It's reasonable to conclude that from the beginning of the exile in 586 BCE, many of those exiled upper classes feared less for themselves than for those left behind. As the years passed, any small hope and compassion for their fellow compatriots left behind would slowly have faded. But a few patriotic exiles clung to that hope; they were obsessed by it. By 562 BCE, twenty-four years had passed since the exile in 586 BCE, and those twenty-four years had to have taken a great toll on the exiles' fellow Hebrew men, women, and children left behind in economic turmoil and hard, desperate times. Desperation inevitably leads to an "every man for himself" mentality. How much longer could the Hebrew people continue to hold together as a people? What options or tools did these concerned, exiled patriots have to encourage their people to persevere under such conditions?

After more than twenty years of deliberating this haunting thought and determining what, if anything, they could do to arrest their people's demise, these determined and noble exiles concluded that they were limited to only two tools: pen and scribe. These were the only instruments that could be used to fight back. Pen, ink, and papyrus were the writers' weapons; inspiration was their ammo, and Genesis through Kings II became the salvo that fought back. By convincing a desperate, down-and-out Hebrew population left in the dregs of Jerusalem that they were a distinct and "chosen" people with a common genealogy, a common history, a common constitution, common traditions, a common purpose, and above all else, a common destiny, these writers/thinkers thought they just may compromise the Babylonian dastardly blueprint for their obliteration.

What they wrote is known today as the Bible—specifically, the Old Testament books Genesis, Exodus, Leviticus, Numbers, Deuteronomy, Joshua, Judges, Samuel I and II, and Kings I and II. (The book of Ruth is commonly and correctly believed to have been inserted later.) The writing of Genesis through Kings II began in 562 BCE and was completed about two years later, in 560 BCE. Nebuchadnezzar's death in 562 BCE most likely prompted the biblical writers into taking this expensive and risky action. Several pens (authors) were involved in the writing of these biblical books. A careful book-by-book analysis will clearly show how they went about achieving their goal of promoting the Hebrews' unique culture and society while their leaders were in exile. With this stately goal in mind, the biblical writers eagerly set out on their mission. They sought only for their people to stand together as one united people during these frightful times; nothing more and nothing less was intended. They were writing in Hebrew for the one lone audience who spoke Hebrew: their fellow Judeans left behind in that ancient conquered city named Jerusalem and the areas surrounding it in 586 BCE. They succeeded

When their biblical books finally reached the Hebrew-speaking audience for whom they were intended, this audience was not sitting in their homes or under trees reading these texts as we sit today reading our books and newspapers. Few if any left behind knew how to read. They were most likely sitting in large groups, listening to the writings being read to them by a reader in specific, designated locations where the limited and expensive biblical scrolls were kept. Rather than viewing reels of movie film with images and dialogue, they were listening to reels of words while mentally visualizing images. Storytelling was an important form of entertainment during ancient times, just as it is in modern times—our times. Listening to a story being read isn't much different from listening to the radio in the not-too-long-ago days before images were added by film and TV cameras. In this case, of course, the biblical writers set out to do much, much more than just entertain their troubled people, they set out to save a people, their people.

The stories told in the Bible aren't much different from fictional stories told today of ordinary good guys and bad guys, or of heroic supermen and superwomen who possess great powers against vicious villains. Like the stories of today, the virtuous stories of the Bible are laced with themes such as sex and vice (or sin) that provocatively entertains. Such entertainment value does prove to hold the audience's attention long enough to drive home the biblical stories' more important underlying messages. Scandalous biblical tales such as the story of Sodom and Gomorrah certainly maintained the audience's rapt consideration while letting their unifying lessons of morality and virtue sink in. Keep this in mind as you consider the biblical authors' literal construction of Genesis–Kings II in the following chapters.

You will see how each book fits neatly with the writers' intended purpose of holding their people together. The first biblical books were written between 562 and 560 BCE, as mentioned, and added to over the centuries. After reading through each chapter, you may very well come to understand the Bible in new and revealing ways under this particular light. The authors of these books died long before they could discover how ultimately great, profound, and historically significant their unintended achievement would come to be.

CHAPTER 7

# Genesis

"In the beginning …" So begins Genesis. In the beginning, the biblical writers set out to construct a common genealogical line connecting all the Jewish people together by blood, in order to keep their stressed-out people bonded during the exile. Before detailing their people's genealogy, however, the writers explained how "God created the heavens and the Earth."

It's necessary to point out that more than a few preexisting creation tales lent themselves to the creation of Genesis's first few chapters. One among them was Egyptian in origin, written near the beginning of their unified history, which had commenced around 3000 BCE and marked the emergence of what is known as Egypt's Early Dynastic period.

Egypt's First Dynasty arose near Memphis, where a burgeoning town formed that eventually became their capitol. The emergence of such a grand town beneath the starry night above the great Nile River assuredly sparked wonder among its many inhabitants, and it was here that ancient Egypt's Memphite Theology of Creation originated not long at all after Egyptian writing had been roughly invented. (Most ancient-near-east historians agree that early alphabets evolved from the symbols used to record economic or business transactions among ancient merchants and traders.)

The Egyptian theology dictates that the Egyptian god, Ptah, came to hold a place above all gods, including "creator gods." It was

He (Ptah) who made all and brought the gods into being … for everything came forth from him, nourishment and provisions, the offering from the gods and every good thing. Thus it was discovered and understood his strength was greater than that of the other gods. And so Ptah was satisfied after he made everything, as well as the divine order.

The creation story in Genesis is similar to the Egyptian theology in important ways. Genesis 2:1-2, for example, says, "Thus the heavens and earth, and all the host of them, were finished. And on the seventh day God ended His work which He had done." A few verses later, God said, "Let the earth bring forth grass … and the tree that yields fruit …" Note again that these first biblical books were written nearly 2,500 years after the Egyptian's Memphite Theology of Creation had been written. (Regarding Ptah, see *The Ancient Near East Volume I: An Anthology of Texts and Pictures*, edited by James B. Pritchard.)

A second and even earlier Mesopotamian creation myth begins,

"They erected for him a princely throne. Facing his fathers he sat down, presiding. Thou art the most honored of the great gods, thy decree is unrivaled, thy word is Anu. … The four winds he stationed that nothing of her might escape … He brought forth Imhullu, the Evil wind, the whirling wind the hurricane."

Several verses later we read they confirmed him in dominion over the gods and the earth:

"Let us make humble obeisance at the mention of his name." "Let his utterance be supreme above and below!" "Let his sovereignty be surpassing and having no rival." "As for us, by however names we pronounce, he is our god!"

Likewise, in the 31 short verses of Genesis's first chapter, we read how a God brought the heavens, the earth, and all its inhabitants into being, along with a man He made in His image. In Genesis 2:4, we read, "This *is* the history of the heavens and the earth, in the day that the Lord God made the earth and the heavens." All He made was good, and all man could freely eat from every tree in the garden—but, He warned his people, should they eat from the tree of "the knowledge of good and evil," they "shall surely die."

The parallels between the Egyptian and Mesopotamian/Akkadian creation myths and those found in the opening chapters in Genesis are too apparent to ignore. Although not as obviously as Noah's flood story borrowed from The Epic of Gilgamesh, the biblical creation story found in the opening chapters of Genesis does reflect the pattern of the biblical writers' occasional use of extra-biblical sources in crafting their work.

These captivating mythical images, borrowed as they were from ancient texts of great civilizations, found their way into the first pages of Genesis for good purpose. The first two chapters of Genesis introduced the Bible, no less, to its specifically targeted audience, launching the biblical project itself. Intertextuality aside, the biblical writers were compelled to draw their lower classes of fellows into their story right up front with entertaining, inspiring storytelling. Creation stories were obviously popular back in those ancient days. Why not bring the creation genre back to their tired, tried, and struggling fellows who could use some good storytelling the most? As you will see, once they had drawn the audience into their story, the biblical writers expertly carried their specifically targeted audience into aspects of the story designed to inspire their people and bond them together. And the writers might as well make *their* Lord the one who created the heavens and the earth—forget Ptah!

So, God created the heavens and earth in grand style and fashion, after which point the biblical writers could begin to quietly educate and instruct, hopefully without losing their audience's interest. Consequently, not far into Genesis, the Lord creates Adam and makes for him a companion, Eve, who brings forth their offspring, Cain and Abel. After Cain kills Abel, Adam's wife gives birth to Seth, and so on and so on. Chapter 5 begins with the genealogy of Adam, whom God made in "His likeness," and called his offspring "Mankind." Adam finally dies at the ripe old age of 930, leaving his son Seth, of "Adam's likeness," to carry on until he dies at the age of 912. Chapter 5 sums up the genealogy of Adam.

In chapter 6 we read, "it came to pass, when man began to multiply on the face of the earth, and daughters were born to them … that the sons of God saw the daughters of men … were beautiful," and mankind became plentiful upon the earth. One such man that came to be born was named Noah who had three sons. Together, this family survives the flood, and Noah's sons' genealogy is summarized in chapter 10. (From earlier chapters in this book and from the creation examples just noted above, one can clearly see how portions of Genesis 1–9 were inspired—*lifted* may be the better term in some parts— from extra-biblical texts that had existed many, many centuries before Genesis through Kings II were written. Regardless, many can argue, this is good storytelling, so what does complete originality really matter, given the grand purpose behind the authors' intent? Nevertheless, many can sensibly and correctly argue that the biblical writers risked raising serious doubt and disturbing questions about the Bible's integrity. Could the bad apple of intertextuality alone spoil the barrel? It certainly may for many, and I find the issue imperative to emphasize and left now for each to consider as they may.)

What was the biblical authors' underlying purpose behind the repeated emphasis on these long, connecting genealogical lines we see so much of in the Bible's first books? It's rather transparent: the authors are instilling within their fellow Hebrews a belief that they all share a common genealogy with these profound biblical characters who supposedly once lived—and it's a genealogy well worth extending, to say the least. In the first few chapters of the first book in the Bible, the writers' Judean audience is repeatedly reminded that "We are of the same blood," a people with a long and glorious bloodline. Obviously, emphasizing such shared characteristics helped drive home the Hebrews' status as a unique and distinct people bonded by blood.

In Genesis 11, we read that the whole earth "had one language and speech," and the "sons of men" built themselves "a city and a tower whose top is in the heavens, let us make a name for ourselves, lest we be scattered abroad over the face of earth." This appears to be a direct reference of the Hebrews' scattered people, those left in Judea and those exiled in Babylon. Additional verses in the chapter go on to describe the Lord as coming "down to see the city and the tower which the sons of man had built" and as "scattering" the people around and "confusing their language" so "they may not understand one another's speech." In other words, this is how the world came to be populated with people speaking different language: by the hand of the Lord.

Now that the biblical writers of Genesis have vividly emphasized their people's long and unifying bloodline, they're now reminding their brothers and sisters left behind in Jerusalem they share a common language too—a common language that defines a people, as does blood or genealogy. This fits well with the belief that through their biblical writings, the writers hoped to encourage their fellow Hebrews, who were left behind in Jerusalem to perish, to find a way to hold on as a people. Soon, the biblical writers will attempt to convince them they share a common destiny too.

A few verses later, Genesis 11:10 turns the text once more toward genealogy, this time beginning with Shem's successors, leading to the birth of Abram after more "begetting" by Terah. Although the birth of Abram began only as a momentous literary event, it was to become a consequential historical event. As Judaism progressed through the centuries, this biblical hero, who reached the ripe old age of 175 years, would eventually be considered the first patriarch of the Judean people.

Abram's story begins earnestly in chapter 12 with the Lord's command to "Get out of your country, from your family and from your father's house to a land I will show you." In Genesis 17:5, the Lord fittingly changes Abram's name to Abraham. The land the Lord commanded Abraham to leave was to the east of Babylon, in ancient Mesopotamia (present-day Iraq), considered the first great civilization known to mankind. Consequently, many people rely on this biblical account as true and believe the Hebrew people originated in ancient Mesopotamia, pushing their history back some thousands of years earlier than that recorded in history books today.

By establishing this command to Abraham, the biblical writers suggest, if not imply, that the Judean heritage reaches all the way back to the very beginning of urban civilized man, and that their ancestors were once members of the great and renowned Mesopotamian civilization.

However, modern archaeology reveals, and ancient Near East historians agree, that the Hebrew people arose in and around Judea during the late thirteenth century BCE, in

Mesopotamia. It's quite possible that oral stories proudly passed down through time may have spoken of Hebrew roots reaching back thousands of years earlier to ancient Mesopotamia. We do know that the biblical writers at least carried that notion forward simply with pen and papyri, with or without a storied tradition. Also, the Hebrew language is one of the Semitic languages, a group of languages that have early roots in Mesopotamia but are clearly distinct from anything ever spoken in ancient Mesopotamia.

While this biblical contradiction with modern archaeology may be a bit unsettling to some, modern Jews of today claiming Canaan as their rightful homeland have a historical foundation. That aside, one thing we all can agree on, according to the biblical story, was that the land the Lord commanded Abraham to travel to was Canaan. From here, many upper-class Jews, including the biblical writers, were taken into exile and resettled in Babylonia while most of their fellow Judeans remained where their forefathers had lived for centuries before.

On behalf of the direly threatened Jewish people at the time, the biblical writers of Genesis had established a Judean genealogy or bloodline, a common language, and a common history reaching all the way back to Mesopotamia by chapter 17. Although archaeology reveals this as fiction, that's beside the point. The writers' purpose for creating it is not. From the biblical writers' perspective, these characteristics are what constitute "a people" worth preserving and strongly holding onto.

Such a people were also worth fighting for, but the writers learned very fast that they were too weak to fight by sword. So they chose to fight by pen—a device often mightier than the sword, as says the popular cliché—in their grandiose effort to prevent the Hebrews' assumed demise precisely prescribed by the Babylonian exile of the upper classes and the disassembling of their people. For that reason, as it's becoming clearer, they wrote Genesis through Kings II. With their biblical writings, maybe, just maybe, their dispersed and leaderless people would not be doomed, and instead hold on and survive as a united and chosen people related by blood, language, and a common history. They certainly must have hoped providence would play its hand too, but hope alone wouldn't do.

Perhaps more important than the role heritage and history may play in maintaining their peoples' unification, the writers' set out to create for their people a common destiny as well. Chapter 17 carries this element of the Hebrews' survival as a people a giant step further by moving it into the divine. After the Almighty Lord Himself changes their patriarch's name from Abram to Abraham, the Lord makes a "covenant" between Himself and Abraham. God promises Abraham, "I will establish my covenant between Me and you and your descendants after you … give you and your descendants all the land in Canaan as an everlasting possession; and I will be their God." They, Abraham's "descendants" who were left behind and leaderless, now have a new leader—and it's none other than their own "Almighty" Lord.

In 17:10 we see for the first time the word "circumcision." In the following few verses, the procedure is prescribed as a "sign of My covenant … for every male child in your generations. … And the uncircumcised male child … shall be cut off from his people." Circumcision was a long-practiced custom in Egypt, but the procedure was used only on pharaohs and their sons as evidenced in an abundance of archaeological and Egyptian literary sources. The historical relationship between the ancient Hebrews and ancient Egypt tilted toward Egypt's benefit. The exiled biblical writers, cut off from their people, were well aware of Egypt's role in their latest plight, and you will later see how little regard the biblical writers held for Egypt during their time in exile. Had circumcision not been an established custom before the exile, it's conceivable that the biblical writers were instrumental in prescribing the procedure, believing that if circumcision was good enough for pharaohs, it was good enough for *every* newborn Judean male as well, not only their kings and leaders.

Whatever the case may be, the custom of circumcision became an identifying feature of the Jewish people. If indeed the biblical writers themselves brought this custom to bear, they could only wait for the day when their people's Egyptian overlords saw every Judean male sporting the same penis as their pharaoh.

Before chapter 17 comes to an end, Abraham obtains a wife, Sarah, and God informs Abraham they will bear a son. The biblical writers offer a rare glimpse of their all-too-evident humanity when writing here that after hearing the Lord Himself tell the hundred-year-old Abraham that he and his ninety-year-old wife Sarah will bear a son, Abraham falls "on his face and laughed …" But the Lord persists in telling them they will have a son, and he will be called Isaac, and the Lord have a covenant with Isaac. This foretold son of Abraham eventually became considered as the second patriarch of the Jewish people, following Abraham.

Shortly after, in chapter 18, the self-amused and exiled biblical writer wrote more about a child being born to the couple advanced in age. A curious dialogue ensued between Sarah and the Lord. Upon hearing a conversation between the Lord and Abraham regarding Sarah having yet another child in old age, Sarah, who has been listening in a nearby tent, laughs to herself and is overheard by the Lord.

The Lord inquires of Abraham why she laughed: "Is anything too hard for the Lord?"

Sarah, who has heard the Lord's inquiry, emerges from the

tent and denies to the Lord that she laughed, saying, "I did not laugh," because she was afraid.

But the Lord says to her, "No, but you did laugh."

There Sarah was, caught in the very human act of fibbing by the Lord Himself. Without another word, the Lord let it go while seemingly leaving Sarah a little embarrassed and humbled.

At this point, "Then the men rose from there and looked towards Sodom." Here we'll find the Lord less compassionate.

In the verses leading up to chapter 19 and the story of Sodom and Gomorrah, Abraham questions, and even lectures, the Lord Himself about destroying a city when the righteous will perish along with the wicked. The Lord assures Abraham he would not destroy the city even for the sake of ten righteous souls. Hard-pressed to find any righteous souls whatsoever in the two cities, He destroys them both but spares Lot.

Earlier in Genesis, we read of the Lord flooding the world because of the "wickedness" that inhabited it, sparing Noah and his creatures. With fire and brimstone, He destroyed Sodom and Gomorrah and the wickedness that inhabited the two cities. What do these biblical writers mean when they use the term "wicked," or "wickedness"?

The Hebrew word's translation in 562 BCE most likely meant selfishness, self-centeredness, little regard for others, and being out for one's self. The biblical writers wanted to hold their people together as one cohesive group during the exile, "wickedness" and selfishness worked against this noble cause. Righteousness, another word often used in these biblical books, is the opposite of wickedness. Righteousness meant practicing goodness toward your fellow man, unselfishness, caring for others. Righteousness is what the biblical authors advocated, and wickedness they condemned. "Righteousness" among the Judeans left on their own in Jerusalem had to prevail over "wickedness" if they were to hold together as one united people.

The Lord made clear to Abraham that He would punish the wicked and save the righteous, a message meant for those left behind, who the biblical writers feared would capitulate to their personal hard times and embrace a competitive "every man for himself" mentality—or worse yet, a neighboring culture. The writers feared that either action would rip their people apart. Fearing this consequence, the writers compassionately promised their people that "goodness" would come from working together, from helping one another. By doing so, the writers hoped to encourage a "together we stand, divided we fall" mentality among their desperate people. Under the present circumstances, their hard-pressed people may be far more inclined to do desperate things to save only themselves instead of each other. This outcome, the biblical writers must have dreadfully feared.

Along with righteousness, the biblical authors promoted another virtue of perhaps even greater necessity in these trying times: sacrifice.

In Genesis we find many examples of sacrifice. The greatest of all is Abraham's (intended) sacrifice of his own son, as commanded by the Lord in chapter 22 as a test of faith. Just as Abraham was about to bring the knife down on Isaac, the Lord, convinced of Abraham's willingness to bear the extreme for His sake, stepped in and stopped Abraham from taking his son's life. Of more significance still is what the Lord tells Abraham next: "I will bless you." Indeed, He did: "I will multiply your descendants as the stars of the heaven and your descendants *shall possess the gates of your enemies* [emphasis added]." Not only is sacrifice in itself a noble, selfless act, but sacrifice has its rewards too. This appears to be a point the authors clearly wanted to make: *Hold together, and your sacrifice will be rewarded.*

Mindful of their defeat at the hands of Babylonia, mindful of their brethren left behind to perish, and mindful of the great sacrifices of these brethren, the writers of these texts tactfully turned sacrifice around and presented it to their abandoned Judean audience as a divine test: *How much suffering and sacrifice are all of you left on your own in Jerusalem willing to endure?* The righteous Abraham set the bar high, passing the ultimate test of sacrifice by demonstrating his willingness to take his own son's life for the Lord's sake. Could those in Jerusalem pass their sacrificial test? If so, the writers suggested, the Lord would duly reward them too. The greater their sacrifice, the greater the rewards they could expect to see, including their own survival as a people.

In chapter 25, Abraham "breathed his last" at the age of 175 and is put to rest by his sons Ishmael and Isaac, and the genealogies of Ishmael and Isaac follow. (Again, there's that bloodline.) Abraham's character, like many if not all characters in these books, is a product of fiction that fulfills a purpose. Abraham's origination in Mesopotamia was a matter of thoughtful intent. Consider again the goals these authors wanted to achieve. Placing the Hebrews' common roots through long lines of genealogy that trace back to the seat of civilized man, Mesopotamia, lends itself to the bonding of a people. The writers' purpose was only to hold their people together during the exile, not to create a new religion per se. Only later did a more formalized religion closely based on these texts form as a stronger, more organized "glue" needed to hold even more diverse and more dispersed groups of Jews together as a people throughout the ages—a subject of further discussion later.

Given the superstitions of modern man, let alone those of ancient times, fictional storytelling would not only have been a popular form of entertainment but a motivational tool as well. You must realize that for the exiled authors of these biblical books in 562 BCE, fiction was their only tool. Shaping it was their genius. The writers knew that stories of love, lust, sin, jealousy, dream interpretation, and miracles would attract, inspire, and hold the attention of those sitting around their storytellers; each topic found its way into the Bible. Humans are human.

In chapter 25, we read of the birth of two twin boys, Esau and Jacob, born in that order to Isaac and his wife, Rebekah. In verse 23, the Lord tells Rebekah, "Two nations are in your womb, two peoples shall be separated from your body; one people shall be stronger than the other, And the older shall serve the younger." Esau was the first to emerge from her womb. "He was like a hairy garment all over ..." Jacob, grabbing ahold of Esau's heel, followed.

Esau was a hunter, a "man of the field," and Jacob "was a mild man, dwelling in tents." Others have pointed out that hunting and camping was thought to be a primitive lifestyle, while living in tents and cooking, as Jacob did, was considered civilized. Obviously, a primitive lifestyle was less likely to be favored by the biblical writers, who were clearly possessors of great wisdom and promoters of civilized, cultural stability. There is no wondering why Jacob came to be considered the third patriarch of the Jewish people, rather than Esau.

The Jacob and Esau story is one of relative length, ripe with tales of deceit, rivalry, and jealousy between the two brothers; prophetic dreams and interpretations; famine; love; sex; rape; revenge; betrayal; and power plays. We also read of the death of Isaac at the age of 180, the Lord's taking the life of Judah's firstborn son, Er, because He thought him wicked, and of course more genealogies. Like Abraham, Jacob eventually journeys to Canaan, "the land where his father was a stranger," and takes the name "Israel."

Chapter 26:2 and a few verses that follow are important to

note. The patriarchal torch is passed from Abraham to his son Isaac. Isaac is commanded by the Lord to avoid Egypt, instead choosing to "live in the land of which I shall tell you":

Dwell in this land, and I shall be with you and bless you; for to you and your descendants I give all these lands ... I will make your descendants multiply as the stars in heaven; I will give your descendants all these lands; and in your seed all the nations of the earth shall be blessed.

Of course the land the Lord was talking about was the land of those whom these biblical books were specifically written for and already living in: Canaan, the so-called Promised Land. Promises were exactly the thing the authors of Genesis through Kings II were making to their brethren in Jerusalem. At the same time, the exiled authors were also telling their fellow Judeans not to go to Egypt, where they would be influenced by Egyptian customs and culture. In later books, you'll see their people being discouraged from adopting and adapting to Phoenician customs and culture too, as the Phoenicians were another great civilization with the potential to lure Hebrews away from their own customs and ways. The biblical authors feared these temptations; the very purpose of the Bible was to hold their people in place and prevent any more lost tribes of Israel. In return, their fiction promised the Judeans much, and indeed this fiction ultimately worked. It was genius.

As we follow the narrative of Jacob and Esau, including the nuances and jealousies among Jacob's wives, Leah and Rachael, and Jacob's struggles with God, the story introduces a new very interesting and important character: Joseph, another son of Jacob's.

Joseph is special, blessed by the Lord, and Jacob's love for Joseph provokes Joseph's brothers' jealousies. Joseph's prophetic dreams are his defining characteristic. One prophetic dream, described by Joseph to his brothers, speaks of the "sun, the moon, and the eleven stars" bowing down to him. Soon, the brothers conspire against him, hatching a plot to kill Joseph and throw his body into a deep pit to cover their crime. After a little debate, Joseph is thrown into the pit alive, and the brothers sit down to lunch. Noticing a band of travelers approaching, the brothers agree there is no profit for them in killing Joseph and decide to sell him to this traveling band of Ishmaelites. Following the transaction, the brothers rip and bloody Joseph's clothes, leaving their father to believe he was torn to pieces by wild beasts. In turn, the Ishmaelites (also called Midianites) sell Joseph in Egypt to an officer of the pharaoh, Potiphar.

Remain mindful that the Judean members of the upper classes who were taken from Canaan and exiled at the hands of the Babylonians pointedly blamed Egypt for their predicament, not the Babylonians. As you read through these biblical books, their contempt for Egypt becomes more and more obvious. At the same time, the exiles' Babylonian hosts were quite accommodating. Due to the plotting of Egypt, the Judeans had been manipulated into taking actions against Babylonia that riled Babylonian anger and provoked their revenge. As the story unfolds after Joseph's arrival in Egypt, the resentment and contempt the biblical writers harbored toward Egypt is clearly and often expressed in their writings, as you shall see.

Potiphar sees that the "Lord is with Joseph," who became a favored and successful man "in the house of his master the Egyptian" and soon the overseer of Potiphar's house; the "Lord blessed the Egyptian's house for Joseph's sake." But intrigue begins soon for Joseph in Egypt. Joseph, "being handsome in form and appearance," becomes desired by none other than Potiphar's wife. Joseph refuses her, and his garment is left in the hand of the seductress as he flees. The scorned wife turns to Potiphar with Joseph's garment in hand and accuses Joseph, "the Hebrew servant," of mocking her and wanting to lay with her. Subsequently Potiphar puts Joseph in prison, where he is treated well because the keeper of the prison sees that the Lord is with him.

As pointed out, Joseph could interpret dreams, a skill thought to "belong to God." Eventually, Joseph interprets the dream of the pharaoh himself, informing him that Egypt will experience seven years of plenty followed by seven years of famine. Thus, the pharaoh's knowledge allows him to prepare for the famine. The pharaoh elevates Joseph over all of Egypt, saying, "only in regard to the throne will I be greater than you."

Following the years of plenty, the famine comes as predicted, and is so severe that it covers the entire earth. Seeing Egypt has grain, Jacob sends ten of his sons there to purchase some. Only Benjamin remains, "Lest some calamity befall them."

Upon their arrival in Egypt, Joseph recognizes his brothers and accuses them of being spies. The brothers do not recognize Joseph, who has disguised himself. The brothers deny being spies and explain to Joseph that one of their brothers has remained at home with their father. Joseph eventually frees all but one, filling their sacks with grain and restoring their money. They are to return to Egypt together with Benjamin to seek the imprisoned brother's release.

Upon the brothers' return to Egypt, Joseph sees Benjamin among them and again extends to all his hospitality. Joseph is told their father, Jacob, is still alive. All the brothers are set free by Joseph, who then runs after them and reveals himself.

Upon hearing that his son Joseph is still alive, Jacob travels to Egypt, leaving behind his home in Canaan and the "famine" infecting it. (Be reminded that the word "famine" likely resembles the conditions in Jerusalem and Canaan at the time the Bible was being written around 562 BCE.) God speaks to Jacob and promises him "a great nation there …" Again we see the biblical writers' promise of hope for their own people suffering the same conditions.

In chapter 47, we read that Egypt has welcomed Jacob's people. Working and living the respectful, civilized life of shepherds who herd sheep and live in tents, the Hebrews prosper in the land of pyramids and pharaohs, contributing greatly to Egypt's economy and earning Egyptian respect. As you read through the biblical books, this attitude among the Jews working in Egypt often surfaces: they consider themselves to be good neighbors—worthy neighbors whose labor helps Egypt prosper and deserves Egyptian respect.

Upon the threshold of his death, Jacob calls his sons together and says, "hear, you sons of Jacob, listen to Israel your father." Jacob addresses his sons individually with words such as, "Reuben, you are my firstborn, my might and the beginning of my strength" and "Judah, you are he who your brothers shall praise ..."—another good example of how highly the biblical writers valued the bonds of family. Soon afterward, Jacob, having reached the age of 147, "breathed his last."

Joseph has his father embalmed in Egypt, a process described in Genesis 50:3 that takes forty days, suggesting that Jacob's remains have been afforded the preparations of the highest Egyptian nobility, including even the pharaoh himself. Per his request, Jacob, the third patriarch of the Jewish people known now as Israel, is carried from Egypt and buried in his homeland of Canaan.

Imagine the sadness that would have run through those listening as the story of Jacob's passing was read, and compare it with the same stroke of sadness that fills us when we watch a dramatic scene of a beloved character's death in a movie or when reading a book. That vicarious sadness comes from our imaginative connection with that character and the story surrounding it. It's a dramatic and emotional feeling that draws us deeper into the story, and it attaches us personally to the story and the character. The biblical writers played on this very same human emotion, and in doing so more deeply attached their audience to their story. When a scene gets to you emotionally, you hold onto it much longer—an effect the biblical writers clearly wished to invoke throughout much of their writing as it served their goal well.

Upon the death of their beloved father, and mindful of their sins toward their brother Joseph, the brothers fear Joseph "will hate us." They ask for Joseph's forgiveness and receive it. "Do not be afraid, for am I in the place of God? ... You meant evil against me; *but* God meant it for good, in order to bring it about as it is this day, to save many people alive." These words appear written specifically for the Judean people down and out in Jerusalem, left behind to wither away while their leaders were exiled. They were being reminded bad things can happen to good people, but the Lord means it as a beneficial thing. There's a divine purpose in all their suffering, and good things will come from it—"hold on and you shall see."

Joseph's character has now served the biblical writers' purpose; "So Joseph dwelt in Egypt, he and his father's household." With their fiction, the writers of Genesis elevated a lowly Hebrew servant to the highest level of the Egyptian governing society, a whisker's hair short of an Egyptian pharaoh. The means of Joseph's ascent, the ability to interpret dreams, had been provided to him by God. The underlying message is this: *From **our** Lord we'll derive our greatest strengths, and the Lord will see us through this very trying predicament we're in.* More important, the depiction of a Hebrew ruling over the great Egyptian state along the great river Nile and all its wealth must have felt glorifying to those who were all too accustomed of being bully-ruled by Egypt.

There is one problem with this: Our historical knowledge

of Ancient Egypt is the most comprehensive of the ancient Near East civilizations. Aided by vast archaeological finds, inscriptions carved in stone, and troves of Egyptian and non-Egyptian literary and historical primary sources, our record of Egyptian rulers is fairly in-depth. Other than in the Bible, no record of Joseph the Hebrew ruling over Egypt has ever been found. Given this, anyone serious about verifying historical facts would rightly conclude that no such ruler had ever existed.

However, none of this was a concern for the biblical writers in their determined and remarkable quest to hold their unique people together. For them, Joseph was literarily crafted as a very important figure with purpose, and as such found a lot of space in Genesis' later chapters. Although only a fictional creation, Joseph embodied a grand example of leadership, cunning, fairness, and intelligence. If a leader such as Joseph can gloriously rule the great Egyptian empire as pharaoh himself, another leader as such is among you today, fellow Jews, and he will arise. Joseph, through fiction, was created to inspire by example one among the many to stand up and possess the confidence of his people, as Joseph did—in Egypt, no less.

Coincidentally, never has an emergent leader been more needed than during the exile. Therefore, the biblical writers wrote much throughout Genesis–Kings II about many and varied rulers and leaders—some bad, some good, and some godlike. Examples of character and leadership are in abundance, found in such biblical figures as Abraham and David, along with many more you will soon discover. Often, the biblical writers were explicit in comparing one leader with another. Even when they were not explicit, their underlying intent was most likely to leave the comparison up to their readers to make. Such traits as wisdom, courage, honesty, and deceit played a fundamental role in the biblical writers' effort to inspire the leadership so badly needed among their un-led, uninspired, tramped-down people who were at severe risk. Genesis's Abraham, Isaac, Jacob, and Joseph provided inspired leadership examples, and many more were to follow in nearly every book to come. Leviticus is the one exception, for it had an overriding purpose, as you will soon see.

In conclusion, beginning with Genesis, the biblical writers in Babylon set out to hold their people together following the Hebrews' defeat by Babylon. Their tool was fiction. Their story was intended to be spread throughout neighborhoods and among their people by the few who could read. Among the luscious stories in the book are lessons and promises, inspiration and entertainment, and above all, a people's belief in themselves. In Genesis, the Judeans are reminded that they are a unique people desperately worth saving; they share a long bloodline reaching back to the beginning of time, and consequently share a common language as well.

Their ancestors were purposely, divinely led from Mesopotamia to a land of their own in Canaan, a promised land. Their path would be fraught with hardship. They were told their sacrifice was a divine test that would shape the Hebrew character and ultimately lead to astounding results. There were righteous people and there were wicked people, and the righteous would prevail. Above all, there was a covenant the Lord had made with their patriarchs, and through those patriarchs, to their people—a unique and most valuable covenant worth cherishing and honoring. In Exodus, the Hebrews' story continues, and these same themes become more enriched … and then some.

CHAPTER 8

# Exodus

After reading the first book in the Bible, one could easily come away believing that Genesis rightfully belongs among those works described as literary masterpieces of fiction. Many biblical scholars believe Exodus is better still.

Exodus begins with a recap of the names of the children of Israel and the deaths of Joseph, his brothers, "and all that generation." Remember, in the mid-sixth century BCE, very few could read, and these books could be reproduced only by rewriting them one at a time by the few scribes available. In turn, these books were read to groups of people. Following a reading, the people would gather again days later to pick up where they left off—thus the recap at the beginning of Exodus to bring them back up to speed with the story.

After six short verses, the book of Exodus is launched in verse 7: "But the children of Israel [Jacob] were fruitful and increased abundantly, multiplied and grew exceedingly mighty; and the land [Egypt] was filled with them." Wow. One can imagine how these underclasses of Judeans left behind in Jerusalem would feel after hearing this tale of their "exceedingly mighty" ancestors. Invoking such pride easily lent itself to the writers' goal of holding their fellow Hebrew-speaking compatriots together during their perilous exile. By claiming the Judeans were once many, mighty, and prosperous in the mightiest nation on earth—Egypt, the very country the biblical writers held responsible for their predicament—the writers provided their people with inspiration to endure. This sort of storytelling lent not only self-esteem to their audience, but also a sense of wonder about what would happen next, especially given their present circumstances, along with hope for something better.

The listeners' wondering was quickly answered. There was "a new king over Egypt, who did not know Joseph" and feared the children of Israel—feared their strength, feared they would join their enemies "and fight against us …" This certainly left the listeners with at least a touch of pride and elation.

Keep in mind that, again, at the time of Nebuchadnezzar's estimated death in 562 BCE, nearly twenty-five years had passed since the exile of the Hebrew upper classes in 586 BCE. The animosity between the Babylonians and the Jews would have softened over that long duration. It would have been a rather simple feat for a few exiles associated with the biblical project, or their agents, to slip away and transport by foot and donkey at least a few completed sets of biblical scrolls to their people left behind in Jerusalem.

So, how did the Egypt of Exodus respond to this potential threat, given the strength of the children of Israel? "… come, let us deal shrewdly with them …" begins verse 10, as these feared people are subjected to "taskmasters" who turn them into slaves. Although Egypt benefits greatly from the Judean labors, the king remains fearful and dismayed over how skilled the typical Hebrew laborer is as he watches them with marvel.

These laborers build such impressive structures "for Pharaoh" including "supply cities, Pithom and Raamses."

Given the engineering skill needed to build the great, majestic pyramids, and the emotional impact of the Exodus writers' fictional account of Hebrew engineering marvels delivered first-class to Egypt that in turn invoked fear within the king, one can only imagine the pride the writers' fellow Hebrews must have felt when hearing this tall tale. The writers' skill and talent in the use of such masterful storytelling to invoke a common pride among a people subjected to such desperate straits was extraordinary. It was necessary too, if their people were to hold together as one.

We also read in Exodus that the more infliction the Hebrew people in Egypt are subjected to, the more they multiply, and the more fearfully they are dreaded by the Egyptian ruler. Was this a message intended to promote family and enlarge the Hebrews' own population, and with it their chances of survival while under their own assault? It seems so to me.

Rather than having the masterful Hebrew slaves build Raamses and such, this unnamed "king of Egypt" subjects the skilled Hebrews to "hard bondage," forcing them to make brick out of mud and straw in a process that requires hard labor, but no skill—the most menial of work. The clear intent of the writers was to incite passionate feelings of disgust toward Egypt among their targeted Judean audience, men and women alike. It's likely some among these common Judeans held their "privileged" Judean leaders responsible for their trying conditions while the exiles lived the good and luxurious life in the beautiful city of Babylon. If this were true, turning the left-behind Hebrews' anger toward Egypt and away from the exiles would certainly serve the writers' grand purpose very well.

As seen, hostility toward Egypt by the exiled writers is abundant throughout the biblical book of Exodus. Again it leads one to wonder why anger toward Egypt, rather than Babylonia, is so aggressively expressed. Babylonians, after all, were the ones who invaded Canaan and exiled their leaders, leaving the remaining Judean population to perish in Jerusalem. Plenty of evidence uncovered by scholars of this period has led a number of ancient Near Eastern historians to believe that Egypt coaxed and prodded the Judeans into taking aggressive actions against Babylon on more than one occasion. In consequence, these actions were aggravating enough to ultimately provoke the Babylonians to raise, feed, and march a large army hundreds of miles, at great expense, to exact revenge upon the Judeans. What other reasoning could the biblical writers have had for hostility toward Egypt?

It is also reasonable to conclude that the Judean leaders felt abandoned by their Egyptian neighbors, who failed to come to their defense after the Judeans had faithfully acted on behalf of Egyptian interests and diplomacy to engage Babylonia with such hostile acts. Such blame on Egypt for the Judeans' plight explains the biblical writers' expressions of anger and disgust toward Egypt that we find throughout their books. Directing their people's anger toward Egypt and away from Hebrew leaders who were duped or coaxed by Egypt into their hapless fight with a resurgent Babylonia also makes sense.

Evidently, the biblical writers wisely kept their female audience in mind, offering judicious nods toward women by writing about brave, fearless, selfless, and compassionate acts by female Hebrews—acts that had momentous and grand consequences.

Jealous of and embarrassed by the skills of Hebrew men, the king of Egypt "spoke to the Hebrew midwives," instructing them, when performing midwife duties for Hebrew women, to kill all newborn sons, allowing only female newborns to survive. However, the midwives refuse, because "The Hebrew midwives feared God" and "are not like the Egyptian women; for they are lively and give birth before the midwives come to them." Confronted with this blatant act of defiance, the pharaoh, ruler of all Egypt no less, backs down before the insulted Hebrew women and modifies his decree. "So Pharaoh commanded all his people, saying 'Every son who is born you shall cast into the river, and every daughter you shall save alive ...'" With this, all women, not just Hebrew women, are to cast their newborn sons into the river while saving their daughters.

It's hard to imagine the pharaoh of Egypt being stoked with so much fear as to have all sons born in Egypt "cast into the river," given that the Hebrew birth rate was "fruitful and increased abundantly." But remember, this is fiction; this is storytelling with a great and overriding purpose behind it. Nothing less was at stake than the future of the writers' people—the focus was most certainly not on providing a recounting of history.

In the first chapter of Exodus, the exiled writers' fanciful, yet powerful fiction tells of an Egypt populated by the "fruitful" reproduction of Jacob's (Israel's) twelve sons and the generations that follow. The Hebrew population in Egypt multiplies, reaching great numbers, filling the country with highly skilled engineers whose building talents rival that of those who built the great pyramids themselves. With this, the exiled writers are essentially telling their target audience in Jerusalem that they are largely responsible for making Egypt the mightiest nation on earth.

Early in Exodus, the exiled writers promise their people they share something much more than just the blood of the great ancient people gloriously spoken of in Genesis. The first hint of that promise appears in verse 17 with the description of Hebrew ancestral women who "feared God" and bravely refuse to submit to the king. This effectively places their Lord above the pharaoh himself, suggesting to the writers' fellow Judeans that they do not need a king to survive their squalor. Someone else would protect and rule over them—someone much greater than a king. The writers would soon stop hinting and begin instructing the Hebrews on who their king was and how to serve him.

The writers were acutely aware of the brutal realities of life their audience faced every day. No king would protect the writers' fellow Judeans from being preyed upon by others and their own. If one were to arise—an unlikely scenario—the Babylonian occupiers would probably throw him in confinement or worse. The writers needed their fellow Judeans to have leaders, but had to be careful with what they wrote—or so one would think.

What the writers of Genesis through Kings II set out to do was create a leader for them using the power of fictional storytelling to accomplish the task. Good fiction—good storytelling—is captivating. Great fiction shapes beliefs and ideas, inspires determination and drive. It entertains too, and these stories certainly entertained the weak, worried, poor, and desperate Judeans who had to have sat enthralled by this story, which stole them away from their hard lives, if only for a few moments. The exiled writers' thinking and execution was masterful, a product of human genius.

Alongside intelligence, another important human trait was clearly present among the writers of Genesis through Kings II: a compassion for their own kind, the tendency all human ethnicities share. In the later chapters of Genesis, we read how the Hebrew Joseph, son of Jacob/Israel, rose to esteem in Egypt. In the second chapter of the book that follows, Exodus, Joseph will be forgotten, lost in the shadow cast by the most towering figure in the Bible, short of the Lord Himself: a guy named Moses. Here, in Exodus, the Moses story begins, and it's a good one.

In the first verse of chapter 2, we read, "And a man of the house of Levi went and took as wife a daughter of Levi." Their future child clearly is to be 100 percent Hebrew and a direct descendent of Jacob, of Israel. But there is a problem. The Egyptian king's fear has inspired him to decree that all male children must be "cast into the river," where they will surely die. In a proud act of a Jewish mother's defiance, the daughter of Levi builds an ark from bulrushes sealed by "asphalt and pitch" and sets her newborn son among the reeds by the river's bank. He is soon discovered by a daughter of Pharaoh, who rescues the boy and has him nursed; he becomes her son. She names him Moses. "And the child grew …" (Exodus 1:10).

Many people are familiar with this popular story originally written for and first heard by those desperate people clinging to a meager livelihood in Jerusalem while their leaders were exiled in a faraway land. They listened closely as the story was being read, certainly pleased when hearing that Moses killed an Egyptian who was beating a Jewish man, and later broke up a fight between two other Hebrews. The message was hard to overlook: *The Egyptians are our foe. Let's stop fighting among ourselves.* When asked by one of these men, "Who made you a prince …?" Moses answers, "Surely this is known." The jealous pharaoh soon learns of this, prompting Moses to flee to Midian, where he finds favor with Zipporah and marries his daughter. They have a son and name him Gershom.

At the end of the chapter, following the death of the king of Egypt, the exiled writers recognized the anguish of their people left behind. "Then the children of Israel groan because of the bondage, and they cried out; and their cry came up to God because of the bondage." "God heard their groaning" and God "remembered" (a curious word to associate with God) his covenant with Abraham, Isaac, and Jacob.

Now comes one line in Exodus 2:25 that brightly illuminates

the thinking of this extraordinary group of men clustered in Babylon, trying to hold their people together during the most trying of times. They wrote, "And God looked upon the children of Israel, and God acknowledged them." With this and what follows, the human minds of these early writers of great fiction created their people's own "God" to rule over them in the absence of the exiled elites, and in doing so, the writers handed the Judeans the leader they so desperately needed.

As argued before, by leaving these underclasses of Judeans leaderless, the Babylonians intended to bring about the Hebrews' demise. With their leaders exiled, left behind with no king to protect and rule over them, the Judeans would simply melt away—or so the Babylonians thought. While nearly all the nobles, leaders, managers, artisans, skilled crafters, and other members of the Judean upper classes carted off to their exile in Babylon happily assimilated to the luxuries surrounding them, a few heroes did not forget their troubled Judeans left behind. With their pens, they set out to save those left behind. One will be hard-pressed to find heroes greater than the exiled biblical writers.

In Exodus 2:25, with that one sentence about God's acknowledgment of the children of Israel, the writers provided hope and assurance to their all-but-forgotten people. With their fiction, the writers delivered a God of their own, a "king" who would watch, protect, and rule over the Hebrews. Little did they know how powerful their stand-in king would ultimately become. We certainly know today how powerful he became— He's still wrapped around us.

However, the exiled writers didn't rely solely on the god their pens had brought forth to save their people. They needed to be very specific with the uniform rules and laws that would help govern the Hebrews, and indeed began writing very specific laws and punishments for the infringement thereof in the second half of Exodus and in books that followed.

Moreover, the exiled biblical writers spun fantastic tales in Exodus that would not only inspire and entertain their audience, but promote belief that such entities exist. In Exodus 3, we see the incorporation of miracles, a telltale sign of fictional writing. As with everything they wrote, the text had an underlying purpose. The demonstration of supernatural powers with the performance of miracles confirmed the presence of an actual real-life supernatural being—a god. With the promise "God acknowledged *them* [emphasis added]" in last verse in chapter 2, the Hebrews left behind in squalor suddenly had something better than a new leader: their own god with the powers to save them. From producing balls of fire to healing the unhealable, fictional writers have been using miracles to arouse, entertain, and stimulate imaginations for millennia.

Those abandoned Judeans gathered around their reader, the very first to hear the miraculous story told in Exodus chapter 3, would soon be carried by their imaginations far away from their awful circumstances and delivered to a beautiful and promising place.

Verse one finds Moses, the shepherd, tending his flock and leading it to "the back of the desert" to the "mountain of God." There he stands before a burning bush, "but the bush was not consumed by fire." Imagine that: a bush in flames that never stops burning—wow! And from that burning bush, the Lord Himself speaks to Moses: "Here I Am"! Such words and imagery were certain to have their intended effect on the exiled writers' audience. With this incredible image planted in the listeners' minds, the writers now have God say to them, "I have surely seen the oppression of my people who are in Egypt, and have heard their cry because of their taskmasters, for I know their sorrows." In verses 16 and 17, God says, "I have surely visited you and seen what is done to you in Egypt: and I have said I will bring you up out of affliction of Egypt to the land of the Canaanites … to a land flowing with milk and honey."

Those listening to the story's portrayal of a down-and-out, oppressed Hebrew people whose cry was heard by their Lord, who then promised to take them to a beautiful place, were meant to find hope and comfort in such a tale, as that was the writers' obvious intent. The biblical writers' desire to ameliorate the suffering of their Hebrew brothers and sisters amid dire circumstances through their storytelling explain these biblical books perfectly. These writers were masters of their work. Their elegant telling of a story of hardship felled upon their ancestors, which mimicked the current suffering in Jerusalem and its eventual resolution, offered not only promise and hope, but entertainment and escape as well.

An important component of the writers' plan was the promotion of their own God for the Hebrews. In verse 18, they're very specific: "The Lord God of the Hebrews has met with us …" Soon after, the audience hears the words, "I will stretch out My hand and strike Egypt with all My wonders … and after that they will let you go." The biblical writers felt it pertinent that their people accept and believe in their God and his powers. Soon, much of their writing would turn toward achieving this goal.

With the final two verses in Exodus 3, the biblical writers promise their less fortunate sisters one more thing all women want for themselves and their families: riches. And they can thank God for it:

"And I will give this people favor in the sight of the Egyptians; and it shall be, when you go, that you shall not go empty handed. But every woman shall ask of her neighbor, namely, of her who dwells near her house, articles of silver, articles of gold, and clothing; and you shall put them on your sons and on your daughters. So you shall plunder the Egyptians."

Many folks have suggested that women are more prone to believing in the wonders and reality of God than men. True or not, this perception doesn't appear to have been lost on the creative minds of the biblical writers, given the amount of female characters woven into their masterful work.

In Exodus 4, we begin to see how strong and powerful this God of Abraham, Isaac, and Jacob really is. Is he strong enough to save the children of Israel—and, by extension, the poor and leaderless children of Israel left behind in Jerusalem who are listening to this story?

In the chapter preceding, we read that Moses is just an ordinary shepherd tending his flock. In the second verse of chapter 4, extraordinary powers are handed over to Moses in the form of a rod. It isn't just any rod, nor anything akin to a contemporary magician's magic wand. It is a grand and great symbol of divine power passed onto Moses by God Himself. In essence, this power has separated God from man, and by this gesture, God essentially makes the mortal man Moses a God himself—a lieutenant-like God.

Miracles symbolizing God's power became an important tool of the biblical writers too. "But suppose they don't believe me or listen to my voice; suppose they say the Lord has not appeared to you," Moses asks of the Lord. Moses is then instructed to throw down his rod, and to his amazement, Moses watches it change into a snake. When ordered to pick up the snake, Moses does so, but it immediately changes back into a rod.

Other miraculous demonstrations follow, including changing a healthy hand into a leper's hand and back, and turning water into blood. Moses is now convinced he is indeed speaking to the God of the Hebrews, and is trusted by the Lord to act on His behalf with powers he himself now possesses.

In chapter 5, Moses, emboldened by the powers the Lord has given him in the rod he holds, confronts the Egyptian pharaoh himself and asks that his people be set free. The pharaoh, not impressed by the god of the Hebrews, refuses and makes their work even more burdensome and menial. A showdown looms. The pharaoh confronts Moses and his brother, Aaron, who also has a rod from heaven. After consulting his "sorcerers and magicians," weaklings compared to the Lord, the pharaoh has his men throw down their rods, which turn into serpents too—but "Aaron's rod swallowed up their rods."

The message the exiled writers were telling their fellow Hebrews with this story is very clear. Their God is stronger than the Egyptian god, and with that power comes the opportunity to punish the people of Egypt for their egregious actions. The biblical writers didn't retreat; they responded with their newly found divine strength. The power of God in Moses turns the Nile waters into blood, killing all the fish and leaving the Egyptian people no water to drink.

But the pharaoh still refuses Moses's request to let his people go. So next, Moses "brings forth frogs abundantly" that fill homes, bedrooms, ovens, and kneading bowls and climb all over the people. The pharaoh asks Moses to rid the land of these frogs, promising to let the people go, and the righteous Moses does as he's asked. Again the wicked pharaoh refuses to honor his word. Now come lice, and then come flies, and finally the pharaoh's submission.

But again the wicked Pharaoh changes his mind and refuses to honor his word. So here come the boils that "break out in sores." Then along comes the hail, the rain, the east wind, the locusts, and the darkness. Still it is not enough; "the Pharaoh's heart hardens" and he refuses to let Moses's people go.

The Lord turns to Moses and informs him that He'll bring a great plague down upon Egypt and with it death "to all the first born of Egypt," from the pharaoh all the way down to their animals. He specifically explains to Moses how the people of Israel are to protect themselves from this plague. This event is called the Lord's Passover. Verses later, the Lord says, "I will have brought your armies out of the land of Egypt," and instructs His people to "observe this day throughout your generations as an everlasting ordinance." Passover remains an important Jewish observance to this day. Creating an annual scheduled holiday for a people to observe and celebrate with specific instructions was a master stroke toward unifying a people, just as the biblical writers set out to do. These writers were determined to do their bit in keeping their people together. One can relate Passover to America's Fourth of July celebration—but on a grander, heavenly scale reaching far beyond the secular.

It's also interesting to note that each of these plagues was an attack on a specific Egyptian god. For example, when darkness enveloped Egypt, it was an attack on Ra, the Egyptians' sun god. The goddess Heket was depicted as a woman with a frog's head; she was said to blow the breath of life into the nostrils of the bodies that her husband, the god Khnum, had fashioned. When the Egyptians' cattle died in Exodus 9, this was an attack on the bull gods Apis and Mnevis and the cow goddess Hathor. The writers' broader and deeper message to their people was, *There's no god like Jehovah.*

This great story of the Hebrews' arduous struggle and ultimate victory over the powerful Egyptians, divinely aided by the hand of their own God, was delivered first-class by the pens of the exiled writers straight to the hearts and minds of their fellow Judeans suffering in Jerusalem. The fact that this never happened was beside the point; instilling a common pride among their audience was not. Fiction works.

Times of great hardship will foster anger, and tempers will rise. Anger among the Hebrews left to perish in Jerusalem was a matter of great anxiety to those trying to promote cohesion among those Judeans. As stated, channeling the Hebrews' anger toward Egypt and away from their own people's role in the blunder craftily advanced the writers' goal of uniting and holding their people together in order to ensure the Hebrews' survival.

Additional stories in Exodus tell of how the Egyptians reduced the skilled and knowledgeable Hebrews to slave labor over the hard and menial task of making mud brick. This sort of degradation was purposely reminiscent of the Hebrews' current stress in Jerusalem during the exile. As Exodus continues, you'll find glorified, uplifting stories of how the Jewish people rose above it, suggesting that exile-era Hebrews stricken with great hardship of their own will rise above it too, as long as they hold on together, for they are the chosen people.

Gratified by the belief that their Hebrew god, the Lord, had prevailed over the Egyptian gods, and pleased to hear of the acts of revenge against the Egyptians for their malfeasance during this long-ago, fanciful time, along with the tale of their ultimate release from their bonds with Egypt, the Judeans must have found the Bible a sweet source of comfort amid dreadful circumstances of their own. The similarities between the Hebrews' fictional long-ago hardships in Egypt and the tough times gripping the writers' contemporaries in Jerusalem were easy for the audience to assimilate, just as the exiled writers obviously intended.

The Exodus story marches on. The children of Israel are free from Egypt and unobtrusively journeying to a new place and a new beginning. But then! Just as the audience had been made to believe the children of Israel were safely on their way out of Egypt, they see "all the pharaoh's horses, his chariots and his horsemen" coming after the Hebrews the very moment they find themselves standing on the shore of a great sea with no escape! What came next has since become one of the most well-known tales to this day, and was surely riveting to that original Judean audience: Moses holds up his rod, the sea separates, and the people make their escape on foot through the divided sea—but not before they see the Egyptian chariots and army coming after them on that same dry land. Verses later, the Lord commands Moses to "Stretch your hand over the sea, that the waters may come back upon the Egyptians." Moses does as he was commanded, and the sea closes up upon the Egyptians and swallows them all. "So the Lord saved Israel."

Chapter 15, which immediately follows, is important to note. It begins with seventeen verses of song. One who imagines sitting among those ancient, stressed-out Judeans listening to this story may begin to feel what they may have felt when the words of this song were first spoken, or sung, or read in tempo to them: "I will sing to the Lord ... for He has triumphed gloriously ... The horse and its rider ... He has thrown into the sea." Verse 11 reads, "Who is like you, oh Lord, among the gods?"

In this moment of great peril, the power of the Hebrew Lord exacts great misery and death on the entire Egyptian army. The point is made again of how powerful the Judeans' Lord can be. A second important point is also made: the "children of Israel" bear no guilt. Their only desire is freedom from forced menial labors, and ask only of the Egyptians their freedom to leave. They are made out to be practical, innocent, honest, and good people while the Egyptians, on the other hand, are made out to be the bad guys. This precept is clearly driven home by the biblical writers—as long as their fellow Judeans left in Jerusalem remain righteous and do not turn to wickedness, of course.

Exodus 17 begins: "Then all the congregation of the children of Israel set out on their journey from the Wilderness of Sin ..." Soon, the children of Israel "thirsted for water," and with a touch upon a stone by Moses's magic rod, the rock pours out water. Their thirst quenched, off they go again. Exodus 18:8 is another excellent illustration of who the Bible's intended audience was, and how the story was designed to encourage them to hold on as one. "And Moses told his father-in-law all that the Lord had done to Pharaoh and to the Egyptians for Israel's sake, all the hardship that had come upon them on the way, and how the Lord had delivered them." This message of hardship and deliverance by the hand of their Lord was obviously intended to foster hope among the Judeans left behind, along with the desire to withstand the same hardship and suffering. The Hebrew people before them had withstood severe privation, and so could they—and their descendants too, don't forget.

Also of great importance in the Hebrews' struggle to survive their dire circumstances was the ability to govern themselves. As inspiring as the Hebrew god penned by the exiled writers may be, the hardscrabble existence of the Hebrews' everyday lives was all too real. The exiled writers knew their people needed more than a hypothetical Hebrew god caring for them if they were to survive their ordeal intact as one united people.

In chapter 18 of Exodus, the writers begin to lay the bricks of a self-governing apparatus intended to fulfill this fundamental requirement. Jethro, Moses's father-in-law, informs Moses that he alone cannot address his many followers' every problem by himself. Verse 18 reads, "Both you and these people who are with you will surely wear yourselves out ... you are not able to perform it by yourself." The writers begin in earnest to instruct the people on setting up their own sorely needed government. Their very survival depended on it.

"And you shall teach them the statutes and the laws ... Moreover you shall select from all the people able men, such as fear God, men of truth, hating covetousness; and place such over them to be rulers of thousands, rulers of hundreds, rulers of fifties, rulers of tens." In chapter 20 are found the famous Ten Commandments, and in the following three chapters, 21-23, are very numerous and specific laws of dos and don'ts that often specify detailed punishments for disobedience. The exiled writers wanted their abandoned people governed by clear and exact laws.

After the Lord speaks to Moses regarding the laws, the people "answered with one voice ... And the words which the Lord has said we will do." In these chapters, you'll read that the Lord is a jealous Lord who doesn't want His chosen people to worship any other god. The Lord also forbids the carving of other gods' images into silver and gold.

Following Moses's forty days and forty nights on top of the mountain, where the Lord harkened him (Exodus 24), the Lord requests in chapter 25 that his children of Israel make him an "ark" resembling something similar in appearance and function to a coffin, with specific details regarding its construction. It was to be approximately 3¾ feet in length and 2¼ feet wide, and His people would carry Him around with. This concept is very similar to that of an Egyptian device designed to transport divine entities.

The Lord also requests the construction of a table with a specific design where offerings will be accepted. The chapters that follow detail the construction of a magnificent tabernacle and altar; the making of garments, tunics, turbans, and breastplates, including a plate engraved with the words "HOLINESS TO THE LORD"; and Aaron being designated a minister and assigned a robe woven to spec as a holy garment. Reverence for the Lord is most important. In chapter 29 are instructions for ministering by priests. Chapter 30 speaks on the use of incense, the collection of monetary and other offerings, and of making ointments from oil, and then concludes with rituals. As God has made the heavens and earth in six days and rested on the seventh, the seventh day is designated as the Sabbath and is reserved for rest. This important subject is found in chapter 31.

The provision of specific dos and don'ts, along with instructions regarding the collection of offerings and management of theological affairs and such, clearly reflects the biblical writers' mission of preserving and promoting their peoples' unique beliefs and customs as an important unifying force. Such specific instructions seem most appropriate when organizing a people's governing apparatus from afar that must rely upon the unskilled, inexperienced members of society to execute. Those left behind to function and survive on their own surely would find these dictates useful, as well as all those who follow after them.

Chapter 32 tells the famous story of the golden calf. The tale of abandoning principle and ideology in favor of the powerful allure of riches has been told in many ways before and since. In the biblical story, Moses's older brother, Aaron, is the culprit. Despite one miracle or demonstration of the Lord's power after another, humans still exhibited that familiar trait of coveting personal wealth, even in the Bible. After seeing that His chosen people "have turned aside quickly out of the way which I commanded," the Lord turns his anger upon his "stiff necked people." Moses quickly intervenes on their behalf and the Lord relents, somewhat, having let only "about three thousand men of the people" fall by the sword that day. Aaron, the culprit, is not among them. The next day Moses orders his people to "consecrate yourselves today to the Lord ..." Nonetheless, the Lord tells Moses, "Whoever sinned against me, I will blot him out of my book." "So plagued the people for what they did with the calf which Aaron made." The Lord's words "blot him out of my book" are strong and threatening. Who among those listening to this story wants to be blotted out of God's book?

The message of this story seems pretty clear: Do not abandon your God to pursue riches; do not worship the proverbial golden calf. The biblical writers were well aware that those Judeans left behind were poor, and their material prospects bleak. Accumulating wealth other than by inheritance is often an individual effort frequently accompanied by good luck and circumstance. Such wealth befalls only the few, and this appears to have been well understood by the biblical writers. If their people were to survive, the masses had to survive. Developing a positive belief among the Hebrew masses in a future worth living as a distinct people would best be achieved by fostering a belief in their own Lord. What else was there?

The vast majority of the writers' targeted audience were hopelessly poor, stuck deep in poverty, and surviving a day at a time. An "every man for himself" mentality was the last thing that would hold the Hebrews together as a people. *Do not worship the golden calf. Worship the Lord instead*—your *Lord*. God, the Hebrews' very own Lord, was something they could all hold onto, something that gave them hope and cause to get through another day. The biblical writers did not set out to save a few with advice on how to get rich, but to encourage them all to hold on, to convince them that the promised land was near and within everyone's reach.

After the golden calf incident is put to rest, the relatively short chapter 33 in Exodus returns the story to its larger theme, the Hebrews' journey to the land promised by the Lord to Abraham, Isaac, Jacob, "and their descendants." Verse 11 is worth noting. "So the Lord spoke to Moses face to face, as a man speaks to his friend. And he would return to the camp, but his servant Joshua, son of Nun, a young man, did not depart from the tabernacle." By this point, the name Joshua, son of Nun, has been woven fairly well into the story. For Moses, to whom the Lord Himself speaks "face to face," his servant Joshua has gained favor. And indeed, the story of Joshua will become a biblical book of its own following Deuteronomy, the last of the five books of Moses.

As we pointed out before, the biblical books Genesis through Kings II were written over a period of about two years, beginning in 562 BCE and concluding in 560 BCE, twenty-four years after the writers' exile in 586 BCE. It is highly unlikely that these heroic biblical writers set out to save their struggling people from extinction in 562 BCE and write Genesis through Kings II with ancient pens and ink, on papyrus, from scratch. The story had to have been conceived and outlined over the months, perhaps even years, previous to its actual undertaking.

Within a few years of the exile, a few men—and quite possibly women too—set about conceiving a plan to hold their people together. Genesis through Kings II ultimately became that plan. In 562 BCE, the writers were prepared to execute it, and the Babylonian king who had exiled them, Nebuchadnezzar, had passed away. As we know now, the writers' plan was destined to succeed (with a lot of unforeseen help from King Cyrus of Persia, as you will see later).

Chapters 34 and onward, until the book's conclusion with chapter 40, repeats, often word for word, the chapters immediately preceding it. Again we see a common thread of using periodic summations of the story to remind an audience of listeners of what was read previously. As pointed out before, the stories told by biblical writers were intended to be read to groups gathered for that purpose. Storytelling was not only entertainment, but a wonderful relief from the Judeans' daily grind. But also keep in mind the primary goal of the biblical writers. That again was to inspire cohesion among those left behind by inventing a fanciful history of their people, creating their very own god, outlining common blood bonds with an ancestry full of great fantastic people, and offering exaggerated tales of the struggle and sacrifice those ancestors endured to make possible the lives of those who sat in rapture around the one reading their work. By doing so, the biblical writers instilled pride among their down-and-out brethren, along with the determination to endure, while providing moments of relief from their desperate daily struggles. The Bible was a remarkable work intended solely for these struggling brethren given the predicament they were in.

The summation of Exodus 34–40 may be a clue to how long a typical public reading was. Most likely, the readers did not go into a reading holding the entire papyri of Exodus, only that which was to be read for the day. If there was a lack of abundant candlelight, the readings would have taken place during the day. On the other hand, if daytime was for surviving and nighttime was for storytelling entertainment, those sitting around the reader would have experienced the mood provided by candlelight. The readers had to have coordinated the readings among their assigned groups, exchanging the limited papyri among them. Each reading may have also included a discussion among the group of listeners following the reading, including questions and answers.

The image the writers left within the minds of their audience at the conclusion of Exodus was a tabernacle crowned by a divine, misty cloud hovering above and brought forth by the hand of the Lord. This cloud prevented Moses from entering, because "the glory of the Lord rested above it and the glory of the Lord filled the tabernacle." Also of interest are the story's rather long descriptions of the tabernacle and its construction.

The tabernacle, dedicated to Hebrew values, learning, worship, and sacrifice, institutionalized a Hebrew religion. Such an edifice would not only become a symbol of the Hebrew people, but also serve as a community center and meeting point. Its mere presence would beg for it.

We see today that the exclusive, custom-made religion extracted from the stories and instructions in the biblical writers' books proved to be a powerful tool for uniting the Hebrews and holding them together throughout the ages. With the religion institutionalized by the tabernacle and subsequent synagogues standing to this day, history ultimately proved the genius behind these writers' successful work.

## CHAPTER 9

# Leviticus

For those who had listened to the great book of Exodus being told, the third book of Moses, Leviticus, may have been a letdown. But the purpose of the biblical book Leviticus is clear. If the people left behind in Jerusalem were to govern themselves during the exile, they needed laws for all to obey. Leviticus was written to fulfill this requirement and derives its name from the "children of Levi." Leviticus is a book of law—a book of law that brightly reflects the times when it was written. If it were written today, it would handily be rejected and considered absurd. Late-night comics would jump all over it. In order to appreciate Leviticus, it's necessary consider the context of the long-ago time when it was written.

The first three chapters of Leviticus describe procedural details of offerings to the Lord, including a bull, turtledoves or young pigeons, grain, and animal parts. The prescribed rituals include the sprinkling of blood around the altar and the burning of carcasses. All sacrifices are to be performed near the altar and received by the tabernacle built for the Lord, where He now speaks to Moses. Payment of a fine of sorts is required from those who "unintentionally" break the decrees of the commandments. The culprit's fine is a bull and the killing of the bull "before the Lord." This is followed by explicit instructions on how the priest will spread the animal's blood around, and the taking of the bull's fat as a "sin offering." Next, the kidneys and lobes, liver, head, legs, hide, and flesh are taken to a "clean place" and burned.

In chapter 5, the biblical writers turn away from offerings and sacrificial procedures and outline crimes and punishments. Offenses include withholding discriminating evidence; touching "unclean" things, including "creeping things"; swearing; human "uncleanness"; and trespassing. Punishments require the payment of fines, including a lamb or a "kid of a goat," two turtledoves or two pigeons, or a "fine flour." Anyone who "commits any of these sins ... even if he doesn't know," is guilty.

Chapter 6 addresses crimes such as robbery, extortion, and false testimony. When theft is involved, the guilty party must return what was taken "plus a fifth." The breaking of some laws may lead to the guilty person being "cut off from his people."

Descriptions of what's "holy," "unholy," "clean," and "unclean" are abundant in the early chapters of Leviticus. The types of meat that can be eaten is also a matter of law found in Leviticus. The meat of an animal that chews its cud and has cloven hooves may be eaten, except for that of a camel. Meat from animals that chew their cud but do not have cloven hooves is considered "unclean" and therefore cannot be eaten. Nor can the meat of animals such as the pig, which has cloven hooves but does not chew its cud. Fish with fins and scales can be eaten, but those "that live in the water" and do not are not to be eaten; they are "abominations." Buzzards, ravens, eagles, vultures, falcons, and bats are off-limits, as are "flying insects that creep on all fours." Yet, insects with "jointed legs above their feet," such as crickets and locusts, are "clean" and can be eaten. One who eats or touches the carcass of an unclean bug becomes "unclean" themselves and remain so "until evening."

A woman who bears a male offspring will be "unclean" for a week and will complete her "purification" in thirty-three days. Those who bear female offspring will be unclean for two weeks and complete their purification in sixty-six days. After they are "purified," the mothers are told to bring a lamb for a burned offering and a turtledove as a "sin offering." Afterward, "she shall be clean from the flow of her blood."

Diagnosis and treatments for leprosy is a matter of substantial detail in chapters 13 and 14. If one is brought before a priest for the examination of a suspicious "swelling, a scab, or a bright spot," specific instructions are provided for the examining priest to follow. "If a man or a woman has bright spots on the skin ... then the priest shall look ..." If it is determined "he is a leprous man ... his clothes must be torn and his head bare, and he shall cover his moustache, and cry 'Unclean! Unclean!'" The leper is to be isolated for up to fourteen days, and his clothing examined to determine if the garments should be burned or merely cleaned.

The treatment prescribed by the Lord in his instructions to Moses for "cleansing" the leprous required the capturing of "two living and clean birds" and taking them to the patient along with cedar wood, scarlet, and hyssop. Next, kill one of the birds in an "earthen vessel over running water." Take the "living bird, cedar wood and hyssop, and dip them and the living bird in the blood of the bird that was killed ... sprinkle it seven times on him who is to be cleansed from the leprosy, and pronounce him clean ..." and then set the living bird free.

Here, the biblical story bumps head-on into the knowledge of our day. Obviously, the Hebrew Lord penned into existence from the Hebrew mind, as enlightened as He was, betrays

"His" all-too-human creator's mind. We know today that leprosy is a bacterial disease cured by antibiotics. But one must be reminded, after Leviticus was written, it would take nearly another 2,500 years and a lot of luck with a bread mold deposit for man to discover the mold's antibacterial extract, penicillin, and developed the germ theory behind the antibiotic. Even more, the biblical procedures for identifying a potential leper, isolating him or her, and washing or burning the patient's clothes is sound judgment. Taking into account the lack of technology such as microscopes that so advanced 20th century medicine, Leviticus may very well have been ahead of its times in treating disease.

A good illustration of such wisdom is found in the next chapter, Leviticus 15. Here, we read the Lord's instructions for Moses, to "speak to the children of Israel on the topic of 'discharge from the human body,'" and the Lord notes that Moses's "discharge is unclean." The biblical writers wisely and caringly provide their people with specific instructions to keep their beds, furniture, and clothes clean by washing them with water, and to wash their bodies with running water. The writers certainly were aware of the valuable solvent properties of water. In addition to defecated and urinated bodily wastes, other "discharges," such as semen and feminine periodic emissions, are specifically detailed in chapter 15, along with instructions for cleanliness. "Cleanliness is Godliness" remains a faithful and correct description of personal hygiene as a fundamental deterrent to disease. The fact that no one less than Moses, the Lord's personal oracle, spells out the Almighty's instructions in Leviticus illustrates how important these instructions and practices were in the minds of the biblical writers.

Leviticus 18–20 extends the Lord's laws into other domains of immorality. Several verses discourage nakedness and implicit sex with a father, mother, uncle, aunt, daughter-in-law, "wife of your brother," "a woman and her daughter," those "near of kin," or a woman in her period of "impurity." It forbids the mating of man or woman "with any animal." Drinking blood is forbidden. Homosexuality and adultery are forbidden; death is suggested as a punishment for both and for those who mate with animals. Death by burning is specified for one who marries his own mother or daughter. The moral restrictions in these chapters are often repeated.

Found in Leviticus 19 are more interesting and notable directives. A few of these are close in form to the Ten Commandments and previous prohibitions regarding lying, theft, fraud, and the worship of idols or molded images. Their people are also instructed not to "glean" their fields and vineyards—rather, let the unfortunate glean them. In other words, when one harvests his agricultural field, he is not to comb, or "glean," through the fields until every piece of commodity is collected. He is to let some of it lie, to let the more unfortunate come behind to "glean" a small fraction of the harvest. There's a good possibility that gleaning had been a common practice prior to the Genesis–Kings II writings. Encouraging such charitable practices is closely in keeping with the biblical writers' ambitious goal of holding their people together during these trying times.

Furthermore, the people are encouraged not to cheat or rob their neighbors, curse the deaf, tell gossipy tales, or take vengeance or bear grudges against their families or community. The biblical writers wanted to discourage dissension among their people; they wanted the Judeans to work together. In verse 19:27, the reader is instructed not to "shave around the sides of your head, nor shall you disfigure the edges of your beard. Tattooing one's skin is forbidden, and one shall not prostitute their daughter causing her to become a harlot." The reader is to honor the "grey headed … the presence of an old man …"

During such hard times as these, people become desperate, and desperate people do desperate things. Yet, the writers have encouraged them not to cross certain lines. Prostituting one's children was one such thing—it was simply beneath the Hebrews, even during such hard times.

Of interest in an earlier verse is a broad command to impose "no injustice in judgment." Also, the biblical writers suggest that "one shall not be partial to the poor or the rich and mighty, but rather treat all the same including strangers." Their codes of conduct also included upright and useful references for one to maintain honest scales and measurements of weight, alongside a range of other conduct guidelines, such as those discouraging one from seeking after "mediums and familiar spirits." Again, one must keep in mind this advice was written nearly 2,600 years ago by comfortable, educated, upper-class exiled Jews on behalf of their poor, struggling fellows with this grand, noble, costly, and risky biblical endeavor while exposing themselves to peril to save their own, unique kind. Are we not, believers and nonbelievers alike, grateful they did?

Chapters 21 and 22 discuss the holiness of priests and rules for marriages. Promoting marriage was important during these dreadful times. Again, consider these rules in light of the writers' overarching goals. They saw an obvious need to advocate customary practices and civility among a people confronted with hardship at every turn.

Leviticus's chapter 26 is where one will find the rewards and punishments exacted by the Lord upon those who follow His laws and those who don't. For those who follow His laws, the Lord promises His chosen people wonderful and abundant rewards—and His wrath and punishments if they do not. For those who obey, the Lord pledges His tabernacle and promises to multiply their people. He promises them rain, fruit, bread, and peace, while their enemies will fall by the sword. "I will walk among you and be your God, and you shall be My people." If they do not follow his laws, the Lord threatens, they will suffer a host of dastardly punishments, including terror, wasting disease, and defeat by their enemies. If you disobey, the Lord says, he will "scatter you among the nations ..."

The exiled writers obviously intended to put the fear of God into their people. Absent a king and state, these left-behind Hebrews needed a governing authority, and that authority here became their own Lord. You'll see how the writers cover their bases in later books by promoting kings too—whatever works. Be it the Lord or be it a king, the biblical writers advocate leadership, coupled with common codes of conduct and anything else under the sun that will help bond the Judeans. The writers knew how easy it can be for a minority population to slowly merge, member by member, into a surrounding culture; they made every effort coding common laws, customs, and practices to help unify their people.

Given the memory of the lost tribes of Israel in the north, it is easier to understand and appreciate the writers' supreme endeavor. This endeavor is the true story, the human story behind the Bible that has gotten lost among the miracles and divine images propagated by religious institutions and pop culture ever since. Despite the obvious human hand behind the Bible, such writings came to be called "scripture" or "scared" writings. This underscores the genius of these biblical writers.

Leviticus 27, the last chapter of the book, is curious in one respect. The chapter is largely dedicated to governing economic monetary and commodity trading exchanges, and is very similar in form to many other chapters in Leviticus describing what's legal and what's illegal.

One must assume these monetary guidelines also fall under the previous divine promises of rewards and punishments meted out by the Lord. Strangely, the chapter appears to be out of place—one chapter ahead of itself. The chapter is formatted similarly to most other Leviticus chapters, with short, precise verses of instructions. chapter 26 reads differently in form and in content, and seems a better conclusion for Leviticus than chapter 27. Throughout Leviticus, specific punishments for infractions doled out by man are common. Chapter 26, by bringing the Lord's ultimate hand into the mix of punishment and reward, fits with the writers' obvious intention of nurturing a fear among their fellow Hebrews of the Lord's wrath. Secular enforcement may be hard to enact following the sort of organizational collapse intentionally brought about by the exile of the Hebrew leaders; provoking a "fear the Lord" mentality among the Judean population left behind is a logical recourse to consider—perhaps the only recourse.

There is a very real possibility that some or maybe much of Leviticus was written before 562 BCE or even before the exile itself in 586 BCE. Incorporating the established codes of conduct and laws that maintain order and foster cohesion among the Hebrews is not only reasonable, but also is clearly in keeping with the ultimate goal of the biblical writers' work. Attaching the glory of their Moses story to such laws carried them beyond secular legal doctrine and into the realm of divine commands. Such laws and their related nuances may have been commonly debated among the educated and knowledgeable who were exiled while the average commoners left to perish more often found motivation from the plainness and candor of religion.

It's worth noting that only four of the first ten chapters dedicated to Moses and the elevation of Aaron's role in the tabernacle begin with the refrain "Now the Lord spoke to Moses, saying …" while all but one of the last seventeen chapters begins with that refrain. It is in these chapters where we find very specific laws, procedures, and punishments that could have been established in coded law before the exile and practiced by the judges, priests, and other professional members of the legal societies who were carted off to Babylon. (The two exceptions are chapters 16 and 17, short chapters that use a less official tone to discuss offerings, sacrifice, and atonement.) Attributing these laws to the Lord via Moses and then invoking a fear of the Lord in chapter 26 seems to make sense, given the stated goals of the biblical project.

Leviticus stands alongside Genesis, Exodus, Numbers, and Deuteronomy, and the five are collectively referred to as the books of Moses. But Leviticus also stands apart in important respects. Using short verses expressing laws and punishments, including banishment and death, Leviticus is largely a book of secular law, of crime and punishment, and much of it was very likely established doctrine before the exile. Hitching it to the Moses story is yet another example of the wisdom of these books' exiled authors. If the Judeans left behind were to survive, they must organize as one people under the same law, practice the same religion, and believe in their own "jealous" God who watched and ruled over them now that those who once had were far away, and maybe gone forever.

CHAPTER 10

# Numbers

Unlike Leviticus, which stands apart from the other four books of Moses, the Book of Numbers fits comfortably well with Genesis, Exodus, and Deuteronomy.

Numbers, the fourth book of Moses, finds Moses "in the Wilderness of Sinai ... on the first day of the second month of the second year after they had come out from the land of Egypt ..." Thirteen months to the day have passed since the chosen people's storied exodus from Egypt, and they now find themselves in a "wilderness," a word that conjures up an uncultivated state similar to that taken upon by the leaderless Hebrew population left behind. Although Egypt is far behind in this part of their story, the Hebrews continue to face a long journey full of trials, tribulations, and challenges on their long trek to Canaan, the Promised Land—a journey that closely mirrors the trials and tribulations confronting their Judeans left behind.

Numbers is a relatively long book among Genesis through Kings II, second in length to Genesis. In a broad sense, the book's message is one of ancestral sacrifice for the betterment of future generations, particularly those generations facing hardships brought upon them by the defeat at the hands of the Babylonians in 586 BCE, and again, this message is very appropriate in advancing the goals of the biblical writers. These glorious fictional tales of ancestral, ordinary everyday Hebrew men and women who took upon themselves heavy and dangerous burdens, including forty years in a wilderness at great expense to reach the Promised Land were clearly expected to uplift, inspire, and encourage their fellow people left behind.

Another message within this story titled "Numbers" is just as clear: if the Hebrews' ancestors could face down and overcome great challenges of sacrifice and hardships lasting a "number" of years, so too could they. This is much of what Numbers is about.

Numbers is yet another biblical Book abundantly dedicated to laws and procedures. The heavy emphasis upon defining common laws that we find in the five books of Moses illustrate not only the importance the biblical writers placed upon the laws' usefulness in maintaining order, but their underlying belief in plain legal directives as a necessary instrument in their quest to develop cohesion among their people. Indeed, the exiles' tools were few, and establishing a common code of law was clearly one. Consequently, common Hebrew law found a prominent place in the biblical writers' work.

Be reminded that these biblical books, Genesis through Kings II, were not distributed as one large scroll. Given the combined length of the twelve books, a single scroll would obviously be much too cumbersome, if not impossible, to construct. Consequently, it's very unlikely that any given listener heard each and every book individually read. With this consideration, the biblical writers, obviously believing the laws were of great importance, felt it imperative to include a broad stroke of laws repetitively throughout their first five books.

The second verse of the book of Numbers begins with the Lord commanding Moses to take a census "of the congregation of the children of Israel" by recording the "number of names" of males "twenty years and above" who would form an army of Israel. From this, the book's title derives its name.

The genealogies of the heads of each of the twelve tribes "from his father's house," beginning with Reuben and ending with Naphtali, are detailed, "and those who were able to go to war" ultimately total 603,530. Establishing a record of genealogies, as we have seen time and again throughout the five books of Moses, is in keeping with the previously stated goal of the biblical writers. Emphasis on the common bloodlines shared by the Hebrew people reinforced the people's unity. Moreover, taking a census and assigning each man a "number" establishes his membership in a common society. With this story, the writers encourage their audience to take such a census as well—something easy to conclude. Disguising this blatant prerequisite for a possible insurrection against foreign hegemony (lest simple resistance proved inadequate) into this mild and seemingly innocent story is yet another stroke of genius. Genius appears to be abundant among the dedicated, talented, and patriotic men composing these books, assuming the biblical writers were all men, of course.

In addition, chapters two and three in Numbers set forth specific instructions for how the Levites and the other eleven tribes will camp, and assigns specific tasks and duties. Detailing camping procedures and providing the practical organizational structure and division of labor necessary for an orderly society to function makes perfect sense, given the underlying purpose behind writing these remarkable books.

Numbers chapters 4 through 9, in keeping with their purpose of repetition, continue with additional monotonous laws and procedures similar to those found in Leviticus. Topics covered in detail include tabernacle and altar procedures, cleansings, offerings, Passover, human discharges, handling and care for lepers, and what to do if defiled by a corpse. Maintaining an altar where sacrificial and other ceremonious acts can be performed is in keeping with the capabilities of those left abandoned in Jerusalem and elsewhere, while building a new tabernacle or rebuilding the glorious tabernacle destroyed by the Babylonians probably was not. Advocating, and providing instruction on, the performance of such Hebrew religious ceremonies before an altar, if successful, would foster Jewish fellowship and bonding. This best explains the biblical writers' inclusion of much detail regarding altar procedures and ceremonial practices.

Chapter 5 is worth a close examination. Here, jealousy and adultery are again on tap for discussion. According to the Lord's law spelled out in Numbers, should a man become jealous over his alleged wife's infidelities, and she is innocent, the man is instructed to go before the priest and deliver an offering to her. If she is guilty of adultery, "the priest shall put the woman under the oath of a curse …" that will make her "thigh rot" and "her belly swell." The woman is required to drink "bitter water" that brings about this curse, "and the woman will become a curse among her people."

It is interesting to note that the laws found in Leviticus prescribe death as the penalty for adultery, not a rotting thigh and swelling belly curse. This lends credence to the suggestion that many of the codes of law found in Leviticus and tied to the Moses story may have been in existence well before the biblical authors of Genesis through Kings II sat down to their work in 562 BCE.

Among those gathered around the reader of these first nine chapters of Numbers, a few, if not more, may have been impatiently listening to many of the same old laws over again. But their interests and attention were soon to be aroused as the reader moved on to chapter 10. Here, with a glorious scene, the story leaps away from laws and back to the ever-trying challenges and never-ending resilience found throughout their people's long and arduous journey to the "Promise Land." Hammered silver trumpets are used to gather the congregation upon "the command of the Lord by the hand of Moses." The trumpeters wailed loudly, and "the children of Israel set out from the Wilderness of Sinai on their journeys …" The combined armies of the twelve tribes suddenly break camp and march forth to meet their enemies.

With the ark of the covenant of the Lord before them, and Moses saying "Rise up O Lord! Let your enemies be scattered. And let those who hate You flee before You," the abandoned, defeated, and destitute Jews listening to the story must have felt a stirring in their imagination, along with an elevated sense of hope, pride, and inspiration. A dreamy vision of an Israeli army of some 603,530 men strong marching toward their enemy could only have been exalting and glorious.

But it wouldn't have lasted long. Just moments later, in the first several verses of chapter 11, they hear their reader speak yet again of complicating, challenging problems that could doom their fate. They listen as the story's heroes succumb to an all-too-familiar growl as "the mixed multitude yielded to intense craving … Who will give us fish to eat? We remember the fish we ate daily in Egypt, the cucumbers, the melons, the leeks, the onions, and the garlic; but now our whole being is dried up …" Hunger must had been tapping on nearly everyone's door in those dark, dreary times following the fall of Jerusalem by the sword of Babylon. During the decades that followed, constant struggle was the usual order of the day, and privation an agonizing, familiar sensibility for the many. Those listening to Numbers likely remembered the fish and leeks dressed in onion and garlic they had once eaten, but now their "whole being" was "dried up," too. The parallel could not be missed. The Judeans listen as the reader reads on.

Moses takes their case directly to the Lord who, surprisingly, finds the issue disturbing. Apparently irritated by the people's fond memories of their happy, candlelit dining days in Egypt, the Lord tells Moses the people shall eat meat "not one day, nor two days, nor five days, nor twenty days but for a whole month, until it comes out of your nostrils and becomes loathsome to you."

After Moses inquires of the Lord whether "flocks and herds be slaughtered for them ... Or shall all the fish of the sea be gathered together for them," the Lord angrily answers, "Has the Lord's arm been shortened?" Apparently not; the Lord's long arm fells game birds from the skies, which fill the beach with "fluttering quail a day's walk on this side ... and that side ... two cubits," or about three feet thick. But after the people spend days and nights gorging themselves, the Lord suddenly strikes them with a plague "while the meat was still between their teeth." Those who succumbed to their craving are buried right then and there! To hell with them!

This message is clear, and its point obvious and direct. With this story, the writers are telling their people, who are staring privation in the eye, *You are suffering, and you are craving things you used to have in abundance but no longer have, just as the biblical wanderers were craving what they once abundantly enjoyed in Egypt.* Moreover, by this point in the biblical story, Moses's followers should have known the Lord had stood with them in the past and will stand with them in the future. Rather than complaining and demanding, the Judeans are encouraged by the story to accept the challenge as a divine test—a hardship they must bear while keeping faith in their Lord. *Food is scarce, but the Lord is omnipresent, and the hungry should hold on to that.* After hearing this story, perhaps the Judeans would go to bed that night with lifted spirits despite their empty stomachs, making their daily challenges more bearable.

Chapter 13 further illuminates the noble intentions that brought them to write these first biblical stories to begin with. Verse 2 recites the Lord's command to Moses, saying, "Send men to spy out the land of Canaan, which I am giving to the children of Israel; from each tribe of their fathers you shall send a man, every one a leader among them." The twelve spies are commanded to "see what the land is like: whether the people who dwell in it are strong or weak, few or many; whether the land they dwell is good or bad; whether the cities they inhabit are like camps or strongholds; whether the land is rich or poor; and whether there are forests there or not. Be of good courage."

The spies return with what appears to be very depressing news. The land "flowed with milk and honey," and the land's people are not weak, but very strong. The land is full of people who are like "giants" with great stature, while the Israelites are like "grasshoppers." The giants' cities are fortified, and there is no way the Israelites can match up against a people "much stronger than us." The Israelites wonder why they left Egypt only to "fall from the sword."

The Lord's response may have been predictable by now for many. A deeply aggravated Lord asks Moses, "How long will these people reject me? And how long will they not believe Me, with all the signs which I have performed among them?" Moses again takes on the role of a middleman; he calms the Lord down, advocates for his people, and argues that if the Lord "was not able to bring this people to the land which He swore to give them … He killed them in the wilderness." What does this say about the Lord? Moses agrees that the Lord by "no means clears the guilty" but asks of the Lord to "Pardon the iniquity of this people, I pray, according to the greatness of your mercy, just as You have forgiven this people, from Egypt even until now."

Numbers 14:3 reads, "Why has the Lord brought us to this land to fall by the sword, that our wives and children should become victims? Would it not be better for us to return to Egypt?" *Certainly not*, many listeners must have hoped within. This story was intended to remind the people left behind that many generations before had endured great hardships and sacrifice so that they may live in this "land of milk and honey." Moreover, Numbers 14 encourages its audience to trust in their Lord; He is powerful and rewards faithfulness and punishes doubters.

The leaders of these people were exiled far off and away, unable to help them, but the Lord was ever present and watching over them—and, just as important, He was judging them by their actions. If they feared the Lord and stayed true to their faith, the biblical writers believed, this would help encourage their people to hold on and move forward together. In other words, united they may stand, divided they may fall. This philosophy is at the center of the writers' purpose for these first books of the Bible as argued here.

As the Numbers story proceeds, the people pick up and continue on with their long journey to the Promised Land under the Lord's guiding hand with a new fire in their hearts and determination in their minds. Their armies grow, and they defeat and conquer the Midianites. They plunder the land and enrich themselves of its bounties—and once again the biblical writers introduce another consequence that compromises the Israelites' victory and progress in reaching the Promised Land.

The people, now in possession of material comforts, become complacent as their riches grow. They no longer want to cross the Jordan; life is good where they stand, on the eastern side of the river. The biblical writers' masterful fiction has created yet another troublesome obstacle between the weary migrants and the Promised Land in Canaan that Moses desperately wants them to enter—and once again, the Lord's wrath will fall upon them. Because of the Israelites' less-than-steadfast belief and desire for gold and material comforts rather than the divine goal of reaching the land that Moses and the Lord seek for them, the Lord "made them wander in the wilderness for forty years, until all the generation that had done evil in the sight of the Lord was gone."

This indeed is a setback, and an awfully strong consequence for choosing material comfort over the Lord's desire. The curse of the golden calf strikes again!

By this time in the narrative, one can imagine the response within the hearts and minds of the audience of listeners taking in this captivating tale. Certainly, the audience believed that their heroic ancestors should put their temporary monetary comfort aside and complete their journey to the Promised Land.

Left hanging, the story would eventually deliver the happy ending the listeners hoped for, but not after many more obstacles, hardships, rebellions, fiery serpents, plagues, sins, and setbacks.

Finally, in Numbers 33, the people break camp and continue their difficult journey of a lifetime, crossing the Jordan into the promise land. The Israelites are instructed to "drive out all the people," and if they don't, these previous inhabitants left to remain "shall be irritants in your eyes and thorns in your side, and they shall harass you in the land where you dwell." With this warning, could the biblical writers have been slyly insulting the occupying Babylonians as "thorns and irritants" just as well? The Lord says to Moses in Numbers 34:2, "Command the children of Israel, and say to them: 'When you come into the land of Canaan, this is the land that shall fall to us as an inheritance—the land of Canaan to its boundaries.'" The rest of the chapter and remaining two chapters define the boundaries; inheritances among the tribes; endowments of land, cattle, and cities; and directives "not to pollute the land." The book concludes with a listing of inheritance laws within families.

Could the biblical writers be cunningly suggesting the land occupied by the Babylonians was a divine inheritance provided to their people, the chosen people—and worth fighting for and taking back? Somewhere between the lines, did the writers plant a seed of thought in the hearts and minds of their people hoping it would nurse conspiracy and ultimately rebellion as a measure of last resort? *If our people are eventually going to perish*, the writers may have thought, *why not go down fighting?* If the writers feared the end—the ultimate death and extinction of their people, the Jewish people—and the only way to prevent their demise was victory in battle, perhaps such an undertaking should be nobly and bravely considered. Given that Nebuchadnezzar was now deceased, the Babylonians may not be up to the fight. If the right time for war had not arrived, the writers may have wanted to ensure that the Judeans would consider it in the future, when the time was ripe. The thought of an eventual victory alone was worth holding on for, and worth the cooperation required among the Hebrews to live together, work together, and survive together.

Of course, this is only speculation. Nonetheless, given the minds of the biblical writers and their purpose for writing these first books of the Bible, the thought must have crossed their minds. After all, their biblical project alone was a conspiracy to begin with. In between the lines, did the biblical writers coyly, stealthily plant the seed that one day could grow into a revolution as a last resort? If revolution was the Jewish people's only chance at survival as a people, we can pretty much be sure the biblical writers would want their people to stand and fight. If such a deeper hidden message was in fact in their writings, their secret was buried alongside them in their graves. As you will see in later chapters, events always supersede history, and then eventually vice versa.

In a clear manner, Numbers was written solely for the Hebrews left behind to perish by Babylonian intent. The biblical writers wisely spoke directly to their struggling people, saying, *The Babylonians were able to destroy your temple, exile your leaders, plunder your wealth, take your belongings, make you poor, make you suffer, and fill your life with hardships. But they cannot take away your identity, your history, or your Lord (and savior)!*

At the time, however, it still remained to be seen whether the Babylonian design could in fact take away the Judeans' future, which was the Babylonians' obvious intent. In Numbers, by utilizing fictional, uplifting, fairy-tale stories coupled with specific laws and instructions, the biblical writers creatively and wisely encouraged their targeted audience to endure: *The setback delivered to you by the Babylonians is just another test the Lord has handed down to us. We stood the same thing down in our past, and we will stand the same thing down today.*

## CHAPTER 11

# Deuteronomy

Although Exodus is the most revered among the five books of Moses, Deuteronomy in several respects is the most curious and interesting. It was clearly the work of a different pen(s) than those behind Genesis, Exodus, Numbers, Joshua, and on through Kings II. Writing alongside the others, the writer of Deuteronomy is plainly in keeping with the shared singular goal all the biblical writers were working diligently toward: holding their people together as a cohesive and viable population who share a common language, traditions, and culture during these brutal and challenging times.

The writer distinguishes himself by using the word "God" more often in Deuteronomy, whereas in the previous books the authors use the word "Lord" more abundantly, although not exclusively. The terms "the Lord our God" and "the Lord your God" are seen a little more often throughout Deuteronomy as opposed simply to "the Lord," which is more commonly used in the preceding books. The difference is slight but noticeable, and worth pointing out.

Deuteronomy ultimately brings the five books of Moses to

a transcendent, inspirational, and glorious conclusion with an ending that leaves all who experience it splendidly overwhelmed with that deep and satisfying human emotion, gratification. With the Hebrews' leaders exiled, Deuteronomy, as with the other books of Moses, places much emphasis on obeying the Lord's commandments and laws. Absent a king, the Lord must serve as the Hebrew leader if the people were to remain unified as one—or so the writers thought. Provoking fear of the Lord as one would foster the fear of a king, the enforcer of laws, makes perfect sense given the goals of the biblical writers. Of practical concern for Deuteronomy's author(s) was the necessity for those left behind to develop the tools and capabilities to govern themselves. Clear directives in how to do so are found throughout Deuteronomy, along with an emphasis upon obeying specific laws—many echoing the other books but obviously written by a different author.

An important distinction between Deuteronomy and the previous four books of Moses are references to Baal, a popular god of the neighboring Phoenicians. Although the book is committed to the Moses story, deterring the Judeans away from the alluring and seductive Phoenician culture and religion was of obvious concern in Deuteronomy as well. One today could find many from the Orthodox Jewish communities found throughout America and Western Europe similarly concerned over the enticement and allure of the inveigling American and European cultures surrounding young Jewish adults living in such places as Paris, London, New York, Los Angeles, and San Francisco.

Deuteronomy brings the five books of Moses to a close, concluding with the death of Moses. Moses's heir apparent, Joshua, begins his ascent in Deuteronomy, and we find his namesake tagging the biblical book that follows. Like Moses, Joshua's biblical character is fictional, as evidenced by his personal conversations with the Lord. As pointed out before, fiction was the tool brilliantly employed by biblical writers as their chosen means of holding their fellow Judeans together as one united people. Indeed, history proved the writers' use of fiction to be a powerful tool in their quest to compromise the Babylonian design for the demise of the Judean people through the pilferage of their wealth, destruction of their temple, and ultimately the exile of their leaders. After all, Jewish societies and synagogues are found throughout the planet to this day.

Although Deuteronomy, like Leviticus and Numbers, is largely a book of law, the book, in similar fashion as the preceding books, makes use of inspirational, make-believe stories of the Hebrews' ancestors overcoming trials, tribulations, and hardships reminiscent of the Hebrews' current distresses. The first verse of Deuteronomy reads, "These are the words which Moses spoke to all Israel on this side of the Jordan in the wilderness ..." The promised land is in view and within reach. After the Israelites have come so far, enduring hardship after hardship and overcoming hurdle after hurdle, the promised land they'll soon inherit sits before them as the Lord's deserved and fitting reward for their sacrifice. In chapter 1:8, the Lord says, "See, I have set the land before you; go in and possess the land which the Lord swore to your fathers Abraham, Isaac and Jacob to give to them and their descendants after them."

A few verses later, after reminding the reader that the Lord has multiplied the Israelite population, the text returns to an area of familiar primacy: the establishment of a governing structure among the population, in keeping with the writers' goal of encouraging self-leadership among the Judeans. As in the previous books of Moses, the people are encouraged by Moses to choose leaders from their tribes, "leaders of thousands, of hundreds, of fifties and tens." Deuteronomy 1:17 begins, "You shall not show partiality in your judgment, you shall hear the small and the great; you shall not be afraid in any man's presence, for the judgment is God's." The message Deuteronomy puts up front is *Choose your leaders. Your previous leaders have been expelled and exiled, and they must be carefully replaced.*

Found in Deuteronomy are many references to the Lord's people wandering forty years "in the wilderness," such as those found in Exodus and Numbers. In Deuteronomy 2:4 we read the Lord "knows your trudging through this great wilderness" for the past forty years.

The book's several references to "forty years wandering in the wilderness" reminds its targeted audience of the many years it has been since the Babylonians entered and overthrew Jerusalem in 587 BCE, the event that created the conditions leading to the rebellion and subsequent exile. What was left behind in Jerusalem and the surrounding areas likely resembled a "great wilderness" of its own. When the completed biblical writings reached the Judean people living in Canaan and slowly disseminated, the older people hearing these stories about forty years in the wilderness could easily connect it with their nearly twenty-five years and counting of living in a pilfered, downtrodden Jerusalem, and with no apparent relief in sight for the next generations coming along. As pointed out before and worth reminding again, "the wilderness" appears as an intended reference to the wilderness-like conditions in Jerusalem that likely existed at the time the books of Moses were being written. It makes perfect sense.

As interesting as that may be, Deuteronomy is largely a book of laws as stated before. Its author(s) surely believed that the book's instructions and laws could aid the very survival of the Jewish people and their culture. Deuteronomy 4:5–6 reads,

"Surely I have taught you statutes and judgments, just

as the Lord my God has commanded me, that you should act according to them in the land which you go to possess. Therefore, be careful to observe them; for this is your wisdom and your understanding in the sight of these peoples who will hear all these statutes, and say Surely this great nation is a wise and understanding people."

It's pretty obvious that inducing pride among the people was a primary endeavor for the biblical writers. This passage was also a good piece of advice meant to bring order among the chaotic conditions threatening the Judeans' society—conditions created by the Babylonians specifically intended to bring about the collapse of the Hebrew people.

Chapter 4's primary objective was to discourage the worshipping of idols or carved images of any type, male or female. These include all animals, be they "winged" or of the kind that "creeps or walks on legs." The people are also directed against worshipping celestial objects such as the sun, stars, moon, and "all the host of heaven," for God has given such objects as a "heritage" to all mankind, while providing his "chosen people" the "nearness of God." Given that previous civilizations, great or otherwise, worshipped celestial objects, this is an important distinction in Judaic religion; the people are directed to worship only their Lord. In chapter 5, the Ten Commandments are found again, owing to the regard the biblical writers held for these important commandments.

In chapter 6 is found yet another familiar laundry list of dos and don'ts, but written by a different pen, or author. People must multiply and love the Lord. They must teach their children to do the same and write their laws on their doorsteps. Those about to cross the Jordan are told they are to do great things, such as build large cities and harvest fields of fruit and grain. Obviously, this makes perfect sense given the deteriorated conditions the biblical writers intended to ameliorate, or make better.

In chapter 7 the Israelites are instructed not to marry other peoples, because the Lord blesses them above all others. Intermarriage would naturally be a big concern among the biblical writers, and most likely was central to the dilution and cultural cohesion of the northern tribes that disappeared, in a manner of speaking. In truth, they didn't disappear; they simply blended in with surrounding cultures while their societies came under external stress and their less-sticky culture gave way to others. Genesis through Kings II was purposely and specifically written to make the Hebrew culture more sticky, or enduring.

In the following chapter of Deuteronomy, the people are reminded of all the great things the Almighty Lord has done for them, such as leading them through the wilderness, and feeding them with manna, "that He might make you know that man shall not live by bread alone," dressing them in garments that didn't wear out, and bringing them into a land "without scarcity" --- all examples found in chapter 8's first verses that are followed by similar blessings the Lord bestowed upon his chosen people.

In chapter 17 the Lord instructs His people, "you shall surely set a king over you whom the Lord your God chooses ... one from among your brethren" and "not set a foreigner over you ..." Given the biblical writers' stated objectives, this makes sense.

Chapter 22 centers on morality and similar codes of conduct. If one should see livestock "going astray," he should bring them back to his owner. Women and men should not wear each other's clothes, an "abomination to your Lord." If one should see a mother bird sitting with her young or on her eggs, "you shall not take the mother with the young." If one builds a house, he's instructed to "make a parapet for your roof" so no one falls from it.

The virtues of virginity and marital fidelity are discussed, along with warnings against rape. Chapters following address such issues as whom you can and cannot charge interest, family law, crimes and punishments, and tithing that would provide material support for a rabbinic clergy—important and crucial agents at the forefront of the effort to keep the Judean people bonded together. Deuteronomy 28 promises all those who follow the laws will be blessed, and those who don't will be cursed. Follow His commandments, and all His blessings shall come your way. Do not follow His commandments, and you will "be defeated by your enemies … your land turned into powder and dust … The Lord will send on you cursing, confusion and rebuke in all you do …" Again, we read remarks that have been made in the previous books.

Deuteronomy 28:47-53 is of particular interest; while it doesn't stray far away from the already familiar, it distinguishes the hand and mind of its own author:

"Because you did not serve the Lord your God with joy and gladness of heart, for the abundance of everything, therefore you shall serve your enemies, whom the Lord will send against you, in hunger, in thirst, in nakedness, and in need of everything; and He will put a yoke of iron on your neck until He has destroyed you. The Lord will bring a nation against you from afar, from the end of the earth, as swift as the eagle flies, a nation whose language you will not understand, a nation of fierce countenance, which do not respect the elderly nor show favor to the young. And they shall eat the increase of your livestock and the produce of your land, until you are destroyed; they shall not leave you grain or new wine or oil, or the increase of your cattle or the offspring of your flocks, until they have destroyed you. They shall besiege you at all your gates until your high and fortified walls, in which you trust, come down throughout all your land; and they shall besiege you at your gates throughout all your land which the Lord your God has given you. You shall eat the fruit of your own body, the flesh of your sons and your daughters whom the Lord your God has given you, in the siege and desperate straits in which your enemy shall distress you."

This is a great example of Deuteronomy's contribution to the overarching goal behind the biblical project. You can easily see for yourself why this book and the others were written: The writers want to compromise the Babylonian design for their people's demise. They want to save their people, and they chose to do so by writing the Bible.

Then along comes chapter 34, which brings the exhilarating, captivating Moses story to an end. Moses, at the ripe old age of 126, "… died there in the land of Moab 'according to the word of the Lord.'" "His eyes were not dim nor his natural vigor diminished." The Lord himself buried Moses in an unmarked grave "… but no one knows his grave to this day." I'm sure some have gone looking for his grave, but it would be as fruitless as looking for Noah's ark. With their pens, the biblical writers created this hero for their desperate people to believe in, as hard as that is for many to accept. But does it really matter? The biblical writers worked their own miracle, and that is the truth.

CHAPTER 12

# Joshua

The book of Joshua seamlessly moves the story forward from the five books of Moses, continuing with the work of the Lord—only now He speaks to the deceased Moses's former assistant, Joshua, just as He had spoken to Moses:

"After the death of Moses, the servant of the Lord, it came to pass that the Lord spoke to Joshua, the son of Nun, Moses' assistant, saying: Moses My servant is dead. Now therefore, arise, go over this Jordan, you and all this people, to the land which I am giving them—the children of Israel."

A few short verses later, Joshua 1:8 reads, "This Book of the Law shall not depart from your mouth, but you shall mediate in it day and night, that you may observe to do according to all that is written in it. For then you will make your way prosperous, and then you will have good success ..." and with that, Joshua became the leader of the children of Israel.

The advice of "make your way prosperous, and then you'll have good success" seems sound, and is especially appropriate during hard times. The Lord's command that His Book of Law shall not depart from Joshua's mouth illustrates the importance the biblical writers placed upon common law as well as on common customs as underlying unifying forces necessary to hold their people together. The passage further promises prosperity and success or material rewards to all those who embrace the laws, again keeping with the goals underlying the biblical writers' work. The message: *Favor in heaven and favor on earth are the rewards for holding on together, just as the Lord wants you to do!* But this message is the product of human genius, not divine communication.

The book of Joshua promptly steers away from law and moves the narrative toward more inspirational, motivating stories designed to encourage a desperate people. "Have I not commanded you?" the Lord asks. "Be strong and of good courage, do not be afraid, nor be dismayed, for the Lord your God is with you wherever you may go." Again, more words clearly intended for the downtrodden Judeans gathered around their biblical reader, listening intently as the reader made his way through the book of Joshua scroll.

In chapter 3, the biblical author of Joshua again sets himself apart from those who penned the five books of Moses. Although miracles are now familiar for those already acquainted with the books of Moses, the miracles found in Joshua seem to eventually take on a flair of their own, as you will later see. But first, near the conclusion of chapter 3, a miracle very similar to Moses's most famous one comes forth:

"When the people set out from their camp to cross over the Jordan with the priests bearing the Ark of the Covenant before the people ... the feet of the priest who bore the ark dipped in the edge of the water ... that the waters which came down from the upstream stood still, and rose into a heap very far away ... so that the waters that went down ... failed, and were cut off; and the people crossed over opposite Jericho."

The Jordan River's waters miraculously "separate," just as

the Red Sea separated for Moses's people, allowing their escape from the pursuing Egyptians. Now the children of Israel can walk through the divided river and enter the promised land, Canaan, as Moses walked through the Red Sea.

Inducing spiritual ecstasy with such stories of fiction is clearly the writers' intent: *The power of the Lord your God is overwhelming, and His power will see us through. We will overcome all adversity standing in our way, be it a sea or a river. First there was Moses, and now there's Joshua. The Lord spoke to both. The Lord's power is ever great.* The writers' hope of holding their people together during the exile stood not only upon establishing common laws, but also upon inspiring stories such as these, and instilling a pure belief in the Hebrews' Lord, their leader. Using miracles to snare their belief in an all-powerful Lord worked, just as the wise biblical writers had hoped. In times so desperate, wishing for a miracle might get the Judeans through another day.

In chapter 5, the practice of circumcision was brought up for a second time. This procedure was a topic near the end of Exodus 4, and again the audience is told of the procedure here. Circumcision was most likely performed by priests or doctors who practiced the medical norms of the day and place. In the first verses of Joshua 5, we read that the sons of Israel who came out of Egypt have not been circumcised during their forty years in the wilderness. Those who crossed the Jordan are ordered by the Lord to be circumcised.

Joshua dutifully "made flint knives for himself, and circumcised the sons of Israel at the hill of the foreskins." Such a feat may have taken Joshua a good while, but in the minds of the biblical writers, this custom was imperative as an identifier of the Jews as a people that could aid the writers' efforts to keep them united as a distinct group with an identity of their own. The writers' apparent concern over the custom may suggest that the procedure had been decreasing in popularity during the years of the exile. Circumcision had come to be an identifying characteristic of Jewish males. Maintaining the custom would certainly lend itself to the writers' goal of preserving the Judean culture.

The stories found in chapter 7 also parallel with the duress in Jerusalem during the exile. In the previous chapter, the Israeli "men of war" took the city of Jericho, and such plunder had the Lord considering a curse that would surely come back and haunt them. In Joshua 7:1, we read of the Lord's anger over the trespass of taking "accursed" items.

In verses following, some spies talk Joshua into attacking the city of Ai with three thousand men, who are subsequently defeated and "fled before the men of Ai …" and "… the hearts of the people melted and became like water." When hearing of this defeat, Joshua "tore his clothes and fell to the earth on his face …"

Shortly after in the narrative, an embarrassed and ashamed Joshua asks the Lord, "Alas, Lord God, why have You brought this people over the Jordan at all … to destroy us? … O Lord, what shall I say when Israel turns its back before its enemies?"

The Lord angrily answers, "Get up! Why do you lie thus on your face?" Incensed over the taking of accursed, forbidden items, the Lord explains, "Israel has sinned … and has both stolen and deceived; and they have also put among their own stuff. Therefore the children of Israel could not stand before their enemies … because they have become doomed to destruction …"

The defeat suffered in the city of Ai certainly appears to be a clear linking with the Judeans' own defeat in 586 BCE by the Babylonians. The Lord's words "doomed to destruction" were meant to warn and rally: "Get up! Why do you lie thus on your face?" seem like words the biblical writers would have the

Lord say to their down-and-out people hurting from the same consequence, a defeat handed to them by the Babylonia.

In another incident over "accursed" items, the Lord instructs Joshua to "Sanctify the people … There is an accursed thing in your midst …" The accursed thing turns out to be gold and silver taken by a man for his personal gain, along with a "beautiful Babylonian garment." The idea of one man being out for himself while all are suffering is contrary to the goals sought by the biblical writers. The biblical writers were obviously advocating a "one for all, and all for one" mentality among their people. An "every man for himself" mentality during these trying times would doom the Hebrew culture.

Notice the vigorous language used in the book of Joshua. "Doomed to destruction" and "sanctify the people" are strong terms. The biblical writers are consistent in hammering home important themes in more than one book. In chapter 7, the theme is again the familiar proposition that when Israel sins, they lose. If they keep with the Lord, they win. Given the situation in Judea following the fall of Jerusalem in 597 BCE and the squelching of their rebellion by the Babylonians in 586 BCE, which resulted in the exile, must Judeans must have wondered whether they, too, were "doomed for destruction." Greed, theft, and personal gain at the expense of others, along with an "every man for himself" mentality during these challenging times, would push Israel over the cliff, the writers feared. If the people were prodded to "sanctify themselves" or undertake acts of kindness toward one and other, such as sharing, helping each other out, adhering to the Ten Commandments and embracing an "all for one, one for all" mind-set, Israel could save itself from demise.

Accordingly, after getting right with the Lord over the accursed item, Joshua has the Lord on his side again in chapter 8. Regrouped and with the Lord's support, the armies of Israel set out to do as the Lord commanded and lay waste to Ai as they have with Jericho. As the story progresses in chapter 10 (or as it came to pass), we read the "king of Jerusalem heard how Joshua had taken Ai … as he done to Jericho." Accordingly, the king becomes fearful of Joshua and forms alliances with the kings of four neighboring cities, but Joshua routs these kings. As they flee, the Lord pelts them with large hailstones "from Heaven, and they died."

This great victory ushers in another miraculous event reminiscent of the River Jordan's waters ceasing to flow and Moses separating the Red Sea. Joshua says, "Sun, stand still over Gibeon: And moon in the Valley of Aijalon." "So the sun stood still, and the moon stopped, till the people had revenge upon their enemies … And there has been no day like that, before it or after it, that the Lord heeded the voice of a man; for the Lord fought for Israel" (Joshua 10:12–13).

What a story! This story of divine victory over Israel's enemies was clearly written for the Judeans still suffering from their own defeat by the Babylonian forces. Such a tale would have landed squarely into their laps and been received with joy by those huddled around their reader in rapture. This narrative must have been very soothing, like easy-listening music to one's ears, as all may imagine. Not only could the Lord work miracles on land, over a sea, and upon a river, but he could also cause the sun in the heavens to stand still.

But of course, this story betrays "His" human creators. We know today that if "the One" were to make the sun "stand still," He would cause the earth to stop rotating. At the time this was written, even the wise biblical writers were taken in by the appearance of the stars and moon all revolving around the earth, as if the earth were at the center of the universe. Today, nearly every elementary-school child knows better.

With that aside, the author's clever use of miracles lent

hope to their people—a commodity in short supply that their struggling Judeans could surely use. These miraculous events must have found their soothing place in the hearts and minds of the Hebrew people, and of many people since.

As the book proceeds, several more kings are defeated and their lands are possessed by Joshua and his followers before "Joshua grew old." Yet much more land remains to be taken. Several of the book's later chapters describe how vast amounts of land were conquered and dispersed among the tribes.

Land acquisition was an obsession in the book of Joshua. In chapter 18:3, Joshua says, "How long will you neglect to go and possess the land which the Lord God of your fathers has given you?" The chapters preceding, 13–17, disperse "the land that yet remains"—and not only land, but cities too. The inheritance of the land was by lot, "as the Lord has commanded," and distributed among all the tribes. In chapter 15 the lot went to the tribe of the children of Judah; in 16, the lot "fell to the children of Joseph," and so forth. In chapter 18 Joshua directed surveys to be completed and boarders established, and in chapter 19, the tribe of Simeon receives their "inheritance." In chapter 20, "cities of refuge" are "appointed" where those "who kill a person accidently or unintentionally may flee there; and they shall be your refuge from the avenger of blood." In chapter 21, cities are essentially dealt out like a deck of cards, because "The Lord commanded through Moses to give us cities to dwell in, with their common-lands for our livestock."

Finally, chapter 23 begins its wrap-up of the book of Joshua. "Now it came to pass, a long time after the Lord God had given rest to Israel from all their enemies … that Joshua was old, advanced in years." The Lord has given them their land, their inheritance. The overarching, unifying, hopeful message of the biblical writers is summed up perfectly by these inspirational and forceful verses in chapter 23:6–13. Read carefully this passage, and you'll precisely see for yourself the clearest example illustrating why these biblical books were written and who they were written for:

"Therefore be very courageous to keep and do all that is written in the Book of the Law of Moses, lest you turn aside from it from the right hand or to the left, and lest so you go among these nations, these who remain among you. You shall not make mention of the name of their gods, nor cause anyone to swear by them; you shall not serve them or bow down to them, but you shall hold fast to the Lord your God as you have done to this day. For the Lord has driven out from before you great and strong nations; but as for you, no one has been able to stand against you to this day. One man of you shall chase a thousand, for the Lord your God is He who fights for you, as He promised you. Therefore take careful heed to yourselves, that you love the Lord your God. Or else, if indeed you do go back, and cling to the remnant of these nations—these that remain among you—and make marriages with them, and go in to them and they to you; know for certain that the Lord your God will no longer drive out these nations from before you. But they shall be snares and traps to you, and scourges on your sides and thorns in your eyes, until you perish from this good land which the Lord your God has given you. Behold this day I am going the way of all the earth. And you know in all your hearts and in all your souls that not one thing has failed of all the good things which the Lord your God spoke concerning you. All have come to pass for you; not one word of them has failed. Therefore it shall come to pass, that as all the good things have come upon you which the Lord your God promised you, so the Lord will bring upon you all harmful things, until He has destroyed you from this good land which the Lord your God has given you. When you have transgressed the covenant of the Lord your God, which He commanded you, and have gone and served other gods, and bowed down to them, then the anger of the Lord will burn against you, and you shall perish quickly from the good land which He has given you."Obviously, these words of warning, encouragement, and prodding were intended for the writers' fellow, leaderless Judeans, who were feared to be drifting away from their heritage and oneness. These struggling people could do little more than look after themselves, one day at a time, and to each his or her own. They were told not to worship other gods, not to marry outside their culture, and to love *their* God. They were told to avoid the allure of other nations, which are like "snares and traps …"

Obviously, the writers' plan of addressing their contemporaries but slyly covering their tracks, so as not to arouse suspicion and possible hostility from their Babylonian hosts, by alluding to a distant past makes perfect sense, given the limitations of the situation the writers were in. The Babylonian design for the demise of the Hebrew people is transparent: demolish their temple, diminish their wealth, exile their leaders, and let their society's decapitated body decompose. The biblical writings lay bare the writers' heroic and intelligent countermeasure of compromise the Babylonians' design by writing the Bible. This is transparent; it explains Genesis through Kings II perfectly.

Before moving on to Judges, it's appropriate to look once more at what archaeology and history tell us about when and where the Hebrew people arose. They appear in the historical record during the latter half of the thirteenth century BCE. The now-famed Merneptah Stele, taking its name after the Egyptian king and dated at 1205 BCE, contains an inscription of a people known as "Israel." The archaeology record where Hebrew artifacts have been found clearly shows the Israelites arising as a people in the land called Canaan—the same region where Jerusalem is found today.

This information may be disturbing for those who want to

accept the tales of Genesis through Joshua as the literal truth. But for others who support the state of Israel, the archaeological record confirms that this is where the Hebrew people originated. Modern-day Israel is their ancestral homeland.

## CHAPTER 13

# Judges

"In those days there was no king in Israel; everyone did what was right in his own eyes"—so says the book of Judges. Nor were there kings in Judea during the exile of the upper and ruling classes, when Judges was written, and this refrain appears in the book of Judges more than a few times. Such a lack of leadership was exactly the point underlying the forced exile imposed upon Judea following their hapless rebellion in 586 BCE.

Judges is among my favorite biblical books. He who wrote the book of Judges seemed to have possessed a grandfatherly knack for storytelling. His inclusion of tales that somewhat reach beyond the book's central purpose may hint that he was an older man who enjoyed entertaining his audience while instructing it. The written work by this talented author's pen appears more independent and lacking in the precise coordination found among the five books of Moses and Joshua.

In fact, the name "Moses" does not appear in Judges. The first verse of chapter 2 reads, "Then the Angel of the Lord came up from Gilgal to Bochim, and said: I led you up from Egypt and brought you to the land which I swore to your fathers; and

I said, I will never break my covenant with you." So, who led the people out of Egypt, Moses or the angel? It would seem as if an "Angel of the Lord" would be an entity less mortal than the mortal man Moses, who died and was buried in Moab, "no one knows where."

Further references in Judges to the "Angel of the Lord" confuse this entity more. Judges 6:21–23 reads,

"Then the Angel of the Lord put out the end of staff that was in "His" hand, and touched the meat and the unleavened bread; and fire rose out of the rock and consumed the meat and the unleavened bread. And the Angel of the Lord departed out of his sight. Now Gideon perceived that "He" *was* the Angel of the Lord. So Gideon said, "Alas O Lord God! For I have seen the Angel of the Lord face to face." Then the Lord said to him, "Peace be with you; do not fear, you shall not die."

The first verse in chapter 1 of Judges asks this question following the death of Joshua: "Who shall go up for us against the Canaanites to fight against them?" The answer is, "Judah shall go up. Indeed I have delivered the land into his hand." Upon reading this, one might expect Judah to be the central figure in Judges. Judah does go up and win a battle with the Canaanites and Perizzites; however, he is soon eclipsed by characters such as Deborah, Barak, Gideon, and of course the even more familiar Samson.

What the Judges narrative does, and does well, is support the all-important goal of the biblical project in its heroic effort to hold the Hebrew people together during the exile. The biblical writers' fear of corrupting influences upon their fellow Judeans spilling over from other city-nations that "the Lord let stand" in Canaan is a matter of anxiety in Judges, as it was in Joshua. If the Hebrew people were wondering why their all-powerful Lord would surround them with alluring and wealthy city-states greater than they, Judges gave them their answer: "so that through them I may test Israel, whether they will keep the ways of the Lord ..." The Angel of the Lord spoke these words: "I will not drive them out before you; but they shall be thorns in your side, and their gods shall be a snare to you."

The greatest source of uneasiness in the mind of the author of Judges came from a neighboring region best known today by its Greek name, Phoenicia. For him the "snare" set by the Phoenician city-states was a matter of most apprehension, and for good reason; warnings of, and references to, the Phoenician god Baal are abundant in Judges, and the entire goal of the biblical project was to prevent a second and all-too-final melting away of the remaining Hebrew people.

The wise writer of Judges knew all too well the allure of the seductive Phoenician culture and their thriving society. Phoenicia had enticed many into the fold during good times, let alone desperate times such as those ravaging the Judeans during the exile, when this author sat down to write his biblical book with extraordinary skill. Masters of shipbuilding, the Phoenicians had flourished for 350 years at the time of the exile (having begun in 1100 BCE), thanks to maritime skill and merchant trading—and the Phoenicians would continue and continued to prosper for centuries more. Phoenicia's superior twenty-two-letter alphabet, from which the Hebrew script had been derived, was a vast improvement over the cuneiform writing system that preceded it. Phoenicia was also known for their coveted purple dyes and Lebanon cedar wood.

Like Israel, Phoenicia fell to Babylonia after the fall of Tyre in 572 BCE, but had embedded a noteworthy and lasting influence upon the impressionable and individual, free-thinking Hebrews not only during the early sixth century BCE, but for centuries prior, particularly in the matter of the Judeans' religious evolution.

A better understanding of Judges will come from knowing

a little history of ancient Israel's relationship with Phoenicia, and the role Phoenicia's religious traditions had upon the development of the philosophy and religion of the ancient Hebrews.

Early Hebrews had accepted and worshipped Phoenician gods who they had earlier adopted from the people of Ugarit (1450–1200 BCE), particularly Ugarit's popular deities El and Baal. The religion of Phoenicia, like all others of the time and place was polytheistic—many different gods were worshipped. The Phoenician gods had a hierarchy. Their top god, El, stood above Baal, but Baal was perceived to be more important and consequential in many ways because of his control over the annual rains and harvests. Baal's association with fertility led to his taking the form of the powerful bull, and he was credited with the creation of mankind. The pleasure of lovemaking and promoting a fertility cult was part of the ancient Canaanite tradition—and, not surprisingly, was naturally considered erotic and joyful among Hebrews alike. Baal's popularity influenced the examples of love and erotica commonly found throughout the Bible.

However, the early god originating from the Hebrews, the Lord, was based on El, not Baal, as seen in the very name of Isra_el_. The Hebrew name for their Lord was "Yahweh" ("YHWH" before vowels were incorporated into alphabets) found phonetically in the word halleluj_ah_, meaning "praise the Lord." The names "Yahweh" and "Lord" are interchangeable.

But old habits die hard, and the Hebrews did to varying degrees acknowledge both El and Baal, the same gods the Phoenicians worshipped. In Genesis 33:20, we read, "Then he erected an altar there and called it _El_hoe Israel [emphasis added]." In Exodus 6:3, we read, "I appeared to Abraham, Isaac and to Jacob, as God Almighty, but _by_ My name Lord I was not known to them." In ancient literature and archaeological remains, we have learned that El's mate was Asherah. In the Bible we also find the pairing of Asherah with Yahweh, the Lord. (For those who would like to read more on ancient Near Eastern history, I strongly recommend William E. Dunstan's *The Ancient Near East*.)

It is not surprising to see a biblical assault on the worshipping of Baal, along with warnings against adopting the Phoenician culture during the exile. Judges 2:13–14 reads, "They forsook the Lord and served Baal and the Ashtoreths. And the anger of the Lord was hot against Israel." With the Judeans' leaders and priests exiled, little traditional influence remained, "and everyone did what was right in their own eyes." What was right in their "own eyes," the author believed, wasn't necessarily right for the greater good of the Jewish people—a well-founded fear. As emphasized in various ways time and again in the Bible, an "every man for himself" mentality does not a people make.

The biblical writers' fear for their people's future as a culture was undeniably warranted, as destroying the Hebrews had been the Babylonians' intent in decreeing an exile of the Hebrew leaders. The biblical writers took it upon themselves to do what they could from their exiled station to compromise this scheme. Lacking bow, arrow, sword, chariot, and army, their only remaining weapon was put to use: the pen. And oh-so-powerful a weapon it proved to be! Upon the Bible rested the Hebrews' future as a unique and united society. Judges, along with the five books of Moses, Joshua, and the Books of Samuel and Kings all fit snugly with this noble purpose. The book's assault upon worshipping the Phoenician god Baal is best understood in this truly illuminating ray of light.

The author of Judges, most would agree, was a very good storyteller. He knows the value of entertainment and the positive effects that such attention-grabbing amusement can have on a group of listeners. Back then, when television and film did not exist, written entertainment was even more valuable than it is now. A great story can be instructional and entertaining at the same time. In Judges are found in ample amount good, inspirational, and memorable stories, and these tales were clearly intended to be passed along by others in time.

The imaginative narrative of the heroine prophetess, Deborah, and her call to arms under the leadership of Barak in opposition to Sisera's chariots, would have been most pleasing to those hearts and minds gathered around the one reading the scroll of this great biblical book. Hooray for the victors as "the Lord routed Sisera and all his chariots and all his army with the edge of the sword before Barak" as Sisera leaped from his chariot and "fled on foot." In chapter 5 is the beautiful song of Deborah and Barak. Its first refrain sings to their leaderless people: "When leaders lead in Israel, when the people willingly offer themselves, Bless the Lord!" At the time this was written, the exiled leaders were missing from Israel, and leadership was exactly what Israel needed the most.

We also read in Judges that following forty years of "rest," Israel once again finds itself under duress after doing "evil in the sight of the Lord." The next heroic tale, found in chapter 6, tells the story of Gideon and his three hundred men. Among the Lord's first instructions to Gideon was to "tear down the altar of Baal your father has, and cut down the wooden image beside it." After seeing that this has been done, the people gather to defend the altar of Baal and demand that Gideon be put to death. But the Lord is with Gideon, who triumphs over those who worship at the "altar of Baal." The Lord tells Gideon He chooses him to save Israel from the Midianites. Following the Lord's passing of a test given him by Gideon involving dew on a fleece of wool, and after having the Lord perform the same trick to produce an opposite result the next day, Gideon is convinced that he indeed should be the one to save Israel, as the Lord has deemed.

Found in the following chapter are more peculiar instructions, this time given to Gideon by the Lord. After the Lord determines that Gideon has too many men, He becomes concerned Israel will claim victory over the Midianites because of their greater numbers, rather than from His hand. He tells Gideon to inform his men that any of those who are afraid may depart. Twenty-two thousand depart, but ten thousand remain—still too many for the Lord. The Lord then tells Gideon to bring his ten thousand men to the water, where they can be observed lapping the water. Those who lap water using their tongues, as a dog would, are sent home; those who lap water by bringing it to their mouths by hand remain. They number three hundred, and these are the men who will march with Gideon into battle after the lappers get their pink slip, so to speak.

A few verses later, Gideon hears of a dream in which a loaf of barley bread rolls into the camp of the Midians and strikes a tent, causing it to collapse. Gideon takes this as a prophecy and leads his men into battle and subsequent victory over Midian.

Chapter 8 closes the story of Gideon out. After "the men of Israel said to Gideon, 'Rule over us, both you and your son, and your grandson also …'" Gideon's reply may underscore the mind-set of not only the book of Judges's author, but several of his fellow biblical writers too: "But Gideon said to them, 'I will not rule over you, nor shall my son rule over you, the Lord shall rule over you.'"

We have seen how the five books of Moses provided the challenged, leaderless, and destitute Jewish population with instructions and laws that might help thwart the deliberate Babylonian plot for their demise. In Judges, the biblical writers also seemed fearful that those with demonstrated leadership qualities would be eliminated or otherwise removed by the Babylonian allies who walked among the Hebrew population. Any natural leader who dared to rise among the common people in such a way as to pose a threat would surely be at risk under the watchful eyes of spies in the area. Establishing a Hebrew Lord and a "fear the Lord" mentality was the biblical writers' answer for the people's lack of a mortal leader (likely prohibited by the Babylonians to begin with).

Following Gideon's death, the Judges narrative turns its attention once again toward countering the obvious and justified fear that the Judeans will embrace Phoenician culture and their god Baal. Intermarriage, deepening dependency on economic ties with Phoenicia, and "to each their own" mentalities, among other undermining influences, posed serious threats to the struggling Hebrew society and culture, prompting those exiled writers to undertake the biblical project. The Hebrew people were seriously threatened with doom, just as the Babylonians intended. "So it was, as soon as Gideon was dead, that the children of Israel again played the harlot with the Baals, and made Baal-Berith their god."

After skillfully crafting this turn of events with his pen, the wise and splendid author of Judges introduced a new character, the dastardly and wicked Abimelech. After receiving seventy shekels of silver from the temple of Baal-Berith, "Abimelech hired worthless and reckless men." His evil included the murder of his brothers—all seventy of them. After Abimelech had reigned over Israel for three years, "God sent a spirit of ill will" against him, and his demise was certain. His humiliating death—at the helping hand of a woman no less—was the author's fitting way of punishing Abimelech's wickedness. After the stone dropped upon his head by "a certain woman" did not kill him, Abimelech asked a young man to thrust his sword into him. The young man obliged.

Over the next several short chapters, Judges's accomplished author entertains with more wonderful and amusing stories. We read how Jephthah defends Israel from additional assorted threats and receives the Lord's reward, followed by stories of several more "judges" who, as indicated in the book's name, judge Israel. But once again "the children did evil in the sight of the Lord, and the Lord delivered them into the hand of the Philistines for forty years." A true hero was needed now more than ever!

Soon after, the author delivers. Judges 13:24 reads, "So the woman bore a son and called his name Samson; and the child grew, and the Lord blessed him." What follows just a few verses later is a tale that would entertain countless generations over countless years, and more to come for sure: that of Samson and Delilah.

The story of Samson and Delilah is a favorite. Originally written to distract suffering Judeans from their daily toil, the tale has entertained multitudes ever since. Many of the story's lyrical words have found their way into songs, with one version made more popular by the latter-twentieth-century band the Grateful Dead—titled, appropriately, "Samson and Delilah."

The tale begins with Samson making a trek to Timnah, and he is bewitched by a daughter of Timnah named Delilah, who is found among the "uncircumcised Philistines." Samson's father has wished for Samson to find a "woman among the daughters of your brethren," but Delilah's allure is too much to resist.

Samson's great physical strength is made known in no small way when he meets a roaring, charging lion. With the spirit of the Lord within him, he tears apart the beast with his bare hands. This was to be only one example of Samson's mighty strength.

The Samson story is also full of sex and betrayal, including deceit at the hand of his lover, Delilah. The story includes enticing riddles, dastardly plots, and ample displays of Samson's great strength. The source of his strength is a matter of most interest to his enemies; it is soon determined that his long hair gives him his strength. After Delilah, conspiring with the Philistines, lulls Samson to sleep, the villainess has one of her conspirators stealthily enter and cut Samson's seven locks of hair. As Samson is now weakened, the Philistines can "put out his eyes" and imprison him.

Then comes the anticipated twist: all listening to the story would just know Samson is too strong to die alone by another's hand. In prison, his hair begins to grow, and his great strength returns. Unaware of the revival of Samson's strength, the Philistines "when their hearts were merry" ask for Samson to be called from the prison "so he may perform for us." The Philistine escorts dutifully take him to the temple, which is "full of men and women." Upon his arrival, Samson asks a boy to lead him to the temple's pillars, so he might lean against them and feel them. As Samson places his mighty hands on the pillars, he calls out to the Lord, asking "strengthen me," and the Lord obliges. His divinely enhanced muscular power is let loose upon the load-bearing pillars. He breaks them in half, bringing the temple down and killing all within, including himself.

This was captivating storytelling at its near best, and the tale certainly has lingered in the minds of all who have heard or read it throughout the ages. One may believe a story as good as this, but the author of Judges was not through with his entertaining narrative. What follow are tales about silver being molded in images and shrines erected for idol worship, perverse acts of homosexuality, and a dreadful, debilitating civil war that arose after the "children of Israel went up against the children of Benjamin." A great battle between the two groups raged at the appropriate location, Baal Tamar, and the "Lord defeated

Benjamin before Israel." Other battles ensued between the two groups, with the Benjamin tribe being "struck down" again. We read, "These were men of valor. ... And the children of Israel grieved for Benjamin their brother, and said, 'One tribe is cut off from Israel today.'" Ultimately, the children of Benjamin "went and returned to their inheritance," and "the children of Israel went and returned to their inheritance."

"In those days there was no king in Israel; everyone did what was right in his own eyes." So reads the final verse in Judges. These words certainly describe the years of Judean travail brought upon them by the Babylonian exile of their leaders, and with these words the great book of Judges ends. Its narrative and messages fit perfectly with the hitherto-stated goals of the biblical project. Its author rests, not knowing how the extent to which his work will transcend time.

## CHAPTER 14

# The Books of Samuel

Before beginning an analysis of the books of Samuel, a few things are worth briefly mentioning. As one may have already noted, the length of the biblical books Genesis through Kings II are about the same, roughly fifteen to twenty pages on average. As we turn to the books of Samuel, you'll notice that for the first time, we have encountered multiple books bearing the same name. There's Samuel I, followed by a second book of Samuel, Samuel II. But when you read the last verses in Samuel I and the first verses in Samuel II, and realize that the passages are seamlessly connected, the books of Samuel appear to have been written as one book and then divided in half for some reason.

The ending verses of Samuel I:

"all the valiant men arose and traveled all night, and took the body of Saul and the bodies of his sons from the wall of Beth Shan; and they came to Jabashand and burned them there. Then they took their bones and buried them under the tamarisk tree at Jabesh, and fasted seven days."

The beginning verses of Samuel II:

"Now it came to pass after the death of Saul, when David had returned from the slaughter of the Amalekites, and David has stayed two days in Ziklag, on the third day, behold, it happened that a man came from Saul's camp with his clothes torn and dust on his head …"

As you see, the Samuel I text flows uninterruptedly into the text of Samuel II. Why? The same question can be asked about the books that follow Samuel, Kings I and II. One explanation for this division may lie in the length limitations of the scrolls in use at the time, as stated earlier. Two scrolls were required to accommodate the length of Samuel and Kings; thus we have Samuel I and II, and Kings I and II. Certainly this is a minor point of consideration, but interesting nonetheless.

Back to the case at hand: with Leviticus set aside, Genesis through Judges offers a fanciful, spiritual history for the writers' fellow Judeans to believe in, while the books of Samuel and Kings offer a fanciful, secular history for them to believe in. These books were clearly in keeping with the overriding goals of the biblical project, and these books' writers were on "the same page" as the authors of Genesis through Judges. The shared goal, again, was to hold their fellow Judeans together as a people while their leaders were exiled. It is also apparent the authorship of Samuel and Kings was closely coordinated with that of the other biblical writers. Whereas the writers of Genesis–Judges set out to stir the hearts and minds of their abandoned people, the Samuel–Kings group of writers appear to have set out to become the inspiration behind the choosing of a king, despite any fears of Babylonian retribution that, in the twenty-five years since the Jewish rebellion against Babylon, had probably softened up noticeably.

It was clear to all that Judea needed leaders—kings to hold the people together. As argued, the point of the exile had been to deprive the Hebrews of leadership. The book of Judges, as you have read, closed out its narrative with the often-repeated line, "In those days there was no king in Israel; everyone did what was right in his own eyes." This is an obvious reference to the chaotic conditions in Judea during the exile years. Therefore, one important, if not overriding, goal of the books of Samuel and Kings appears to have been a smart and noble effort to at least kick-start a movement toward establishing a leadership structure among the people. While most of the exiled Jews began new and prosperous lives in the beautiful, bustling city of Babylon, a few unselfish, heroic, and compassionate souls undertook this grueling writing project at great expense with a "united we stand, divided we fall" attitude. At a minimum, these writers hoped their work would help ameliorate the dire straits gripping Judea and its people. At best, the writers' grand design would unite and hold the Judeans together as a great people far into the future.

One giant of a problem for their people wasn't Goliath; their problem was that they had been left leaderless. Judea was desperate for any kind of leadership at this time, and the biblical writers knew it. The books of Samuel and Kings address their need for leadership with the telling of tales about Israeli kings past—some good, some bad, some downright evil. All were used to impress the stricken community in Judea enough to prompt a few to ask, "Who among us could rise up and become our king? Who among us is fearless enough, brave enough, and wise enough to stand face-to-face with our Babylonian overseers and negotiate on our behalf?" Judea needed kings, not judges—leaders capable enough to inspire, unite, lead, and negotiate for the people.

Like the group of writers who had set out to propagate an impressive fictional religious history of Israel, the group of writers working on the books of Samuel and Kings set out to create an impressive fictional secular history of Israel. In Samuel, we read how Israel was ruled by different and numerous kings—some good and some bad, reigning during good times and reigning during bad times. The writers hoped their people would learn from the "history" of these largely make-believe kings. They hoped to inspire a gifted and brave few to rise up and lead their subjects, providing the people with the confidence necessary to fulfill their longings and fostering belief in a presumptive and fulfilling future as a united people, society, and culture.

Before proceeding with an analysis of Samuel and Kings, recall once again that the archaeological evidence shows the Hebrews first arising in Canaan in the late thirteenth century BCE from their humble beginnings as sheepherders. But instead, a biblical portrayal of the Hebrews' supposed great paternal ancestor, Abraham, has him arising in the resplendent Mesopotamian civilization, a civilization clearly and highly respected not only by the biblical writers but all ancient Near East historians and their students to this day. The story of Noah saving his people from the flooding by the construction of a large ark is very transparent in its Mesopotamian origin. Moreover, we see Abraham's subsequent ancestral offspring become leading citizens of the great Egyptian civilization, with Joseph being one of Egypt's most celebrated kings. Although outlandish, the tale affords great pride and conceit among the biblical writers' down-and-out people. Ideas that instill such attitudes easily trump truths, including the Hebrews' more unassuming beginnings as Canaan sheepherders, during such challenging times as these, when the Judeans' very future as a people was at severe risk.

The books of Samuel gained fame over the millennia for their story of one King David. Next to Moses, David is the most written-about character found in Genesis through Kings II.

Before turning to extra-biblical sources regarding David,

let's consider again the "Children of Israel's Exodus out of Egypt." References to this event in Samuel underscore the importance placed upon it by the biblical writers who have concocted this whimsical story of their people's exit out of Egypt, complete with an onslaught of Egyptian mounted warriors and a miraculously separating sea. With this story, the writers sought to directly impact the hearts and minds of the Judeans. Why? Because it helps glorify the Hebrews as a great, bold, and determined people whose earlier generations made great sacrifices for the betterment of future generations. Their ancestral sacrifice of "forty years in the wilderness" way back when was now worth paying back with the sacrifice of those left on their own during those trying years of the exile. If their forefathers could survive forty years in the wilderness, at least some of them must have reasoned, they could face down the now decades-long exile and emerge from it intact and with great glory, just like those before them.

Moreover, Judean anger and contempt for Egypt at the time was well-founded. As you may recall, it was Egypt who persuaded, if not coerced, the Judeans into their folly of challenging Babylonia and its king, Nebuchadnezzar, an incident that proved a supreme debacle directly leading to the Babylonian sacking of Jerusalem and its surrounding settlements in 597 BCE. Eleven years later, similar plotting and duplicitous dealings with Egypt led to a second Judean undertaking of yet another feeble and failed rebellion against Babylon's continued occupation. It was this defeat that brought about the Hebrew leaders' exile in 586 BCE, which left the Hebrew population in dire circumstances and prompted the biblical project. The Judeans' troubles all started with Egypt, who played them like puppets during their calamitous conflicts with Babylonia. The story of the exodus from Egypt and similar biblical passages expressing contempt for Egypt played harmoniously with the Judean hearts and minds that detested the Egyptians.

Of even greater significance, at the time when the Bible was being written, large numbers of desperate Hebrews were providing the Egyptians with low-skilled and low-paid labor for such menial tasks as making mud brick. Times in Canaan were not just tough—they were extreme. Moreover, demand for low-skilled labor was strong in Egypt, especially during this time in their history, which is known today as the Saite revival period of 664–525 BCE. It was during these times when the first books of the Bible, Genesis through Kings II, were composed (from 562–560 BCE).

The Saite period was a time when Egypt was flourishing while the Judeans were floundering and severely at risk. Although the menial work was certainly degrading and dreadful, one can expect to have found scores of destitute Hebrew laborers constantly making the trek to Egypt to find work there, particularly during the excruciating times of the exile. The contempt the hard-laboring but proud Hebrews must have harbored for the Egyptians at this juncture helps explain the purpose behind the biblical writers' capricious but uplifting accounts of the proud children of Israel's mass exodus out of Egypt. Leaving the Egyptian scoundrels high and dry of their much-needed hard labor would have inspired great joy and pride among the Hebrews of the day—if only they could! But they couldn't; they were stuck. Life for most Hebrews holding on in Judea couldn't have been much worse.

The books of Samuel tell the story of David. Most biblical, religious, and historical scholars place the odds of David being a real-life king of Israel at 50 percent. These relatively high odds are primarily due to one extra-biblical reference found on what is known as the Tel Dan Inscription in the Israelite city of Dan. The victory stele had been erected to mark a military success over Israel. Found on it is a reference citing "The House of David" in Judea. The stele is dated approximately 840 BCE, far less than two hundred years after King David's assumed long reign had begun, and more than three hundred years before the biblical writing project commenced. The inscription points toward one named David as a historical figure and further suggests he was a man of fame, a leader of Israel with some renown.

However close this may be to proving a King David did in fact exist (which I lean toward), the Samuel narrative is certainly an embellished, if not completely make-believe, account of the popular king. Recording history was definitely not the intent of the biblical writers, as should now be abundantly clear; Herodotus they were not, saviors of the Jewish people they were. While Genesis–Joshua was being written by a closely coordinated group of writers, and Judges most likely by a lone writer with some but little coordination with the Genesis–Joshua group, the books of Samuel and Kings were being composed by a third group of writers working in cahoots with the others. This third group took a separate, more secular tack by addressing the Hebrews' need for leadership, for a king.

The book of Samuel derives its name from a minor character, the "prophet" Samuel, whose part diminishes as the narrative proceeds. Rather than being an "Angel of the Lord," Samuel is a mortal prophet who receives his instructions from the Lord and faithfully redirects them to his subjects. The book of Samuel entertains more than it instructs; diversions from the daily grind, it surely provides. But its greater intent was to precisely deliver its primary goods: the qualities to look for in a leader. As the scroll was read and the story made its rounds through the population, the work would hopefully accomplish its intended effect—to inspire would-be kings to stand up and lead, mimicking the kingly examples found in the Bible.

The book begins with a husband, Elkanah, and his two wives. One of his wives, Hannah, has no children, "for the Lord had closed her womb." The other wife of Elkanah, Peninnah, is jealous toward her rival because Elkanah shows more favor toward Hannah, giving "double the portion" to her that he gives Peninnah. In turn, Peninnah "provoked her severely, to make her miserable …" In return, Hannah turns to the Lord for solace.

Hannah's prayer, which begins in chapter 2, is intentionally perfectly suited for those oppressed in Judea:

"My heart rejoices in the Lord … I smile at my enemies … The bows of the mighty men are broken, And those that stumble are girded with strength … Those who were full have hired themselves out for bread, And the hungry have ceased to hunger … The Lord kills and makes alive; He brings down to the grave and brings up. The Lord makes poor and makes rich; he brings low and lifts up. He raises the poor from the dust And lifts the beggar from the ash heap, to sit them among princes and make them inherit the throne of glory. For the pillars of the earth are the Lord's, and He has set the world upon them. He will guard the feet of his saints, But the wicked shall be silent in darkness. For by strength no man shall prevail. The adversaries of the Lord shall be broken in pieces; From heaven He will thunder against them. The Lord shall judge the ends of the earth."

The prayer then concludes with these words: "He will give strength to his king, and exalt the horn of His anointed."

This is a powerful beginning for the book of Samuel. These great words of promise are more than encouraging; they are uplifting, plainly written for the men, women, and children left destitute in Judea by the Babylonians.

Soon into the text, the antiheroes, the Philistines, make their entrance. Interesting parallels can be drawn between the

Philistines and the Babylonians. Chapter 4 has Israel and the Philistines aligned against each other in several battles.

Verse 2 reads, "Then the Philistines put themselves in battle array against Israel. And when they joined battle Israel was defeated by the Philistines, who killed about four thousand men of the army in the field." A few verses later, after gathering their courage following their initial fear of the Israeli god who "struck the Egyptians …" the Philistines hand Israel "a very great slaughter," killing "thirty thousand foot soldiers" in the Israeli army. To add insult to casualty, the Philistines also cart off the Israelis' "ark of God," presumably with the "Lord" encased within. The news causes Eli the priest to "fall off his seat backward" and break his neck, causing his death.

Seven months later, after the Lord strikes the Philistines several times with "tumors" transmitted by rats, the Philistines decide to get the ark back to the Israelites, but make sure it doesn't arrive "empty." The Philistines include within the ark a "trespass offering" of "five golden tumors and five golden rats," hoping the gesture will relieve the plague of tumors placed upon them.

When the ark arrives, Samuel "spoke to all the house of Israel." He pleads with them to "return to the Lord with all your hearts" and the children of Israel to "put away the Baals and Ashtoreths and serve the Lord only." More than a few biblical writers were dreadfully worried about the influence and pull of Phoenicia upon the Judeans. Glorifying the Lord over the Baals and Ashtoreths makes perfect sense, given the stated overriding aim of the biblical project.

Philistine presence in the Canaan area flourished in the late twelfth century BCE forward until being conquered by the Assyrians around 700 BCE. Remember, the Philistines were the supposed rascals that Samson took down with himself as told in the book of Judges. The biblical writers used the Philistines as the bad guys whom their fellow Judeans could easily relate to the Babylonians. The last thing the writers wanted was to be accused of fomenting resistance and rebellion against Babylon.

Before David's rise into kingship and fame, Saul is chosen king. Chapter 8:22 reads, "So the Lord said to Samuel, 'Heed their voice, and make them a king.'" Nothing could be more obvious to those in Jerusalem as to what their exiled leaders desired them to do. But how should one decide whom to make king? The Judeans were to decipher the clues, and read (or, in their case, hear) between the lines. The writers' wisdom is found in the scroll, which depicts the examples set by the kings anointed by the writers' pens.

Interestingly, a Benjaminite, a member of one of the rebellious tribes defeated in Judges, rose up. Why? Because "There was not a more handsome person than he among the children of Israel. From his shoulders upward he was taller than any one of his people" (Samuel 9:2). His name was Saul. In verse 17, the Lord says to Samuel, "There he is, the man of whom I spoke to you. This one shall reign over My people." Saul's response to the seer, Samuel, is, "Am I not a Benjaminite, one of the smallest tribes of Israel, and my family, the least of all families?" Several verses later, in the following chapter, there is a second reference to Saul's height. "… and when he stood among his people, he was taller than any of the people from his shoulders upward." In 10:24, after remarking again about Saul's height, Samuel himself says, "there is no one like him among all the people." "So all the people shouted and said, 'Long live the king!'"

As it turns out, he didn't live much longer, this king chosen by his height. As one may predict, Saul's reign ended in failure. Moreover, a grieving Samuel hears his "Lord," no less, admit to the mistake. In 15:11 the Lord admits, "I greatly regret that I set up Saul as king, for he has turned back from following Me, and has not performed My commandments." The last verse in the same chapter ends with, "and the Lord regretted he had made Saul king over Israel." In other words, Samuel's all-too-human writer passes his all-too-human faults onto the Lord by setting Him up to fail—putting the Lord, of all entities, into a situation of having to soul search His ridiculous blunder.

As humorous as the Lord's admitted and hapless mistake may be for many, it's more important to appreciate the process Samuel's author is attempting to convey to fellow Judeans in choosing their leader. This is a crucial theme woven into the books of Samuel and Kings: the writers are guiding their compatriots through the crucial process of choosing leaders they so desperately need. Physical stature by itself qualifies no one to lead. A big, tall guy may stand out and have presence, but that says little about his leadership potential.

So what does speak of leadership talent, according to the prophet Samuel? Supposedly, these qualities are found in the writers' caricature of David, the king of Israel—if in fact the book's author intended for him to be their "model king." This appears certain given the length of the David story found in the Bible, second only to that of Moses. What is also certain about the book of Samuel is that its story of King David is not an historical account of a real King David (if one should even have existed), nor was it intended to be. The concept of recording history per se didn't come along until Herodotus's time, 484–425 BCE, one hundred years after Samuel was written. Just like the authors of the other biblical books writing alongside one another, the authors of Samuel and Kings wisely used fiction to achieve their grand design.

1 Samuel 16 is where David makes his entrance onto the pages of a book that would endure for thousands of years to come. Samuel's search for a new king begins after the Lord

sends Samuel to Jesse, a Bethlehemite, where he'll find a king "among his sons." So that Saul will not discover Samuel's treasonous mission, the Lord instructs Samuel to cover his tracks by convincing Saul he's making a sacrifice to the Lord with a heifer. This may indicate the writer's concern about the possibility of Judeans bringing unwanted attention by openly searching for a king, which could be perceived as a direct challenge to the rule of Babylon; some stealth may have been thought necessary.

Shortly after, Samuel makes a selection, and the Lord, apparently after learning from His past mistake, says to Samuel, "Do not look at his appearance or at his physical stature, because I have refused him. For the Lord does not see as a man sees; for man looks at the outward appearance, but the Lord looks at his heart."

After several of Jesse's sons "pass before Samuel," one remains: "the youngest, and there he is, keeping the sheep." David soon becomes the "anointed one," and the "spirit of the Lord came upon David from that day forward ... But the spirit of the Lord departed from Saul ..." With this story, Samuel's writer is suggesting to his fellows in Jerusalem that their king can be found among sheepherders or among menial laborers, or among the people next door. If the Lord is in the selected person's heart—the Lord, not Baal—that person can rise up and lead. The writer's message: *A king is among you. Start looking.* But such a king must embrace the Hebrew's Lord as the imagination of the biblical writers created Him to be.

Not long after, David is anointed, fights his now-famous duel with the giant Goliath, and wins. With the Lord in his heart and a slingshot in hand, David brought down the armored, sword-carrying "Philistine giant." Or was Goliath in fact the Babylonian giant present among them? As Humbaba was the darkness of the forest, was Goliath the darkness of

Babylon? The exiled writers in Babylon dared not say so. They let the parallel speak for itself:

"This day the Lord will deliver you into my hand, and I will strike you and take your head from you. And this day I will give the carcasses of the camp of the Philistines to the birds of the air and the wild beasts of the earth, that all the earth may know that there is a God in Israel. Then all this assembly shall know the Lord does not save with sword and spear; for the battle is the Lord's, and He will give you into our hands."

With these words, the writer or writers of Samuel concede that the swords and spears of the Babylonian occupiers cannot be defeated by force. They encourage resistance by simply holding on while keeping faith in the Lord. Time is needed—a most necessary commodity the biblical writers are trying to buy for the Hebrews. This land has been the home of the Hebrews for centuries and is a foreign land for the Babylonian occupiers. They have to hold on, and stories of Jewish heroes like David, whose inner strength allowed him to slay giants, were intended to encourage the Hebrews to persevere.

Many generations have come and gone since the epic story of David and Goliath was written for their struggling, down-and-out Hebrews. We have all related to this story in several different personal ways. But for those poor and endangered Judeans, the story hit much closer to home. An inspiring story it was, but in the morning, they were still left with their daily grind of slaying a giant with a slingshot.

"Now there was a long war between the house of Saul and the house of David. But David grew stronger and stronger, and the house of Saul grew weaker and weaker." After David's rapid rise to stardom, Saul predictably becomes jealous of him—so much so that he seeks to kill David. But even Saul's son Jonathan sides with David. The jousting between a more mortal Saul and a less mortal David, brought on by Saul's jealousy and urge for revenge, eventually unhinges Saul. David remains upright, spares Saul's life, and defeats the Amalekites. The Philistines are painted as dastardly villains. In the end, Saul is defeated in battle and falls on his sword. The Philistines decapitate Saul, leaving a rather vivid image of the biblical character. Adding insult to injury, they hang Saul and his armor in the temple of the Ashtoreths. Local inhabitants hear of this and remove his body from the wall, bury his bones under a tree, and then fast for seven days.

The first book of Samuel would have lingered with its audience long after its reading, leaving them with a hero, their own King David, and more of his story to look forward to. After the Hebrews heard the first book of Samuel read to them, the echo of the story would have certainly provided all with at least some relief from their never-ending daily slog.

2 Samuel seamlessly keeps the narrative of 1 Samuel flowing. It begins with Saul's large, kingly shadow over David in retreat (if there ever was one) and with David returning "from the slaughter of the Amalekites." The first chapter ends with David's "lamentation" for Saul and his son Jonathan. "… Saul and Jonathan were beloved and pleasant in their lives, and in their death they were not divided …" Not only a sweet homage for these two memorable biblical characters, this expression of Saul and Jonathan's compassion and care for each other would have encouraged the same communal bonding and brotherhood among the hard-pressed Judeans during these destitute times.

The lines "I am distressed for you, my brother Jonathan; You have been very pleasant to me; Your love to me was wonderful, Surpassing the love of a woman" has conjured up theories of homoeroticism among some people today, but this is unlikely the interpretation of the people living during those times. Friendship is wrapped in many different packages, no matter what era it blossoms in. We all can relate to tough times when friends are needed the most, and that hasn't changed nor ever will. If there ever were tough times, they were unfolding during the years the Bible was being written.

In 2 Samuel, Saul is dead, and David becomes king. It's not surprising to find conflict between the "house of Saul and the house of David" and "civil war" between the two groups to ensue. Following Abner's urging with the elders, it will be David who prevails. "For the Lord has spoken of David, saying, By the hand of My servant David, I will save My people Israel from the hand of the Philistines and the hand of all their enemies."

Again, memories and stories passed down of the malfeasance at the hands of the Philistines that occurred in Israel two hundred plus years before Genesis–Kings was written weren't much of concern for the here and now. The obvious connection between the long-ago Philistine scoundrels and the present Babylonian occupiers was pretty apparent. At the time, Israel's leaders were carted off to Babylon while the Babylonians were still at their gate. With this story, the biblical writers were questioning who was going to be king, and a leader was chosen. Perhaps it was time for the Judeans to consider doing the same. It's doubtful the Babylonians occupying Jerusalem would permit a king that ruled over the remnants of Judea, but a leader could be established nonetheless.

As king, David sets out to bring back the ark and succeeds. Soon after, in chapter 7, the Lord makes David "a great name, like the name of the great men who are on the earth," bringing the Babylonian King, Nebuchadnezzar, to mind. "Moreover," the Lord says, "I will appoint a place for my people Israel, and will plant them, that they may dwell in a place of their own and move no more, no shall the sons of wickedness oppress them anymore, as previously." These words seem very appropriate for the current situation in Judea in 562 BCE. The writers further suggest, "When your days are fulfilled and you rest with your fathers, I will set up your seed after you, who will come from your body, and I will establish his kingdom." Chapter 7 continues with this talk and encouragement through to its end. Again, if such writings came to be known to the writers' host, the Babylonians (few of which could read Hebrew script), the "Philistines" would be their cover.

2 Samuel's entertaining and thought-provoking narrative moves forward with tales of Nathan's rebuke of David for taking the life of Uriah the Hittite and making Uriah's wife his own; Joab's scheme for Absalom's return and his subsequent murder; David's flight from Jerusalem; Sheba the Benjaminite's revolt against David; and David's ultimate triumph. The story of King David is brought to an end with a verse from "David's song of Deliverance" and the poetic "David's Mighty Men." From the latter are found these words:

"He who rules over men must be just, Ruling in the fear of God. And he shall be like light of the morning when the sun rises, A morning without clouds ... But the sons of rebellion shall all be as thorns thrust away, Because they cannot be taken with hands. But the man who touches them must be armed with iron and the shaft of a spear, And they shall be utterly burned with fire in their place."

This is certainly good advice for a potential king in waiting.

But the books of Samuel are not quite finished yet; they leave their people with one last chore. Picking up on the important project advocated in the book of Numbers, David is commanded by the Lord to "Go number Israel and Judea ... Now go throughout all the tribes of Israel, from Dan to Beersheba, and count the people, that I may know the number of the people." When the people are counted, they're reminded of their membership, their belonging to a community that speaks a common tongue and shares a common culture. Some Judeans might have packed up their donkeys and journeyed north to Phoenician city-states, believing their families could find more bread there, but they were still members of the Hebrew people, to whom they ultimately owed their loyalty.

The books of Samuel found a comfortable place in the writers' scheme to compromise the Babylonian design for Judea. Leaders were needed to rise up among the people, and the books of Samuel certainly attempted to encourage just that. These books were followed by a second pair of books, appropriately titled Kings.

CHAPTER 15

# The Books of Kings

The books of Kings open with an aging King David "advanced in years." A man named Adonijah steps forward and "exalts himself," seeking to be David's replacement. He is described as "very good looking," but appearance is not a qualification for kingship, as the biblical writers wanted to point out to the leaderless Judeans. Consequently, it was David's son, Solomon, who became king after David's death was recorded in the book's second chapter. Prior to his death, David's instructions for Solomon was for him to "keep the charge of the Lord ... His statutes, His commandments, His testimonials, as it is written in the Law of Moses ... If your sons take heed of their way ... you shall not lack a man on the throne of Israel."

These pointers were again, of course, meant for those made leaderless by the Babylonians. Restoring leadership was an important goal for the writers, an absolute necessity if their Southern Kingdom in Judea was to avoid the fate of their northern kingdom, Israel, which had endured military defeat and melted away into surrounding societies and cultures decades before. The codes of law found in the five books of Moses were to become the Judeans' constitution. The "brave" King David example of leadership found in the books of Samuel was followed with yet another instructional example for a real king in waiting to aspire to, the "wise" King Solomon.

One of Solomon's first acts was to make a treaty with Egypt, perhaps implying that the Judeans should consider using diplomacy to counter the Babylonian occupation, now twenty-five years old and possibly mellowing out a bit. *Let bygones be bygones, and move forward into your future.* (If this were the case, we see the author or authors of Kings advocating a different diplomatic tack toward Egypt, and his attitude found its way into the Bible.)

Solomon also marries the pharaoh's daughter. While some evidence points to David being a historical king whose life has been heavily embellished and even fictionalized in Samuel, the tale of Solomon marrying the pharaoh's daughter definitely points to his being a purely fictional king.

Our understanding of Egyptian history, greatly enhanced by numerous archaeological discoveries and numerous scripted writings in the many tombs and pyramids found throughout Egypt, does not include the Hebrew Solomon whatsoever. Once again, fiction was the writers' tool; their purpose for writing Genesis–Kings wasn't to record history, but to save their fellow Jews from the same fate as the northern lost tribes of Israel.

Solomon's second act is to preside over a dispute involving two harlots (prostitutes) who both claim motherhood of the same baby. What else is a king to do? This popular biblical tale of Solomon deciding the matter by cutting the baby in half, leading one to beg for the baby to be spared and handed to the other (therefore indicating the real mother), leaves Solomon remembered as the wise king. With this, the biblical writers suggest wisdom as a valuable quality a king should possess. "And all Israel heard of the judgment which the king had rendered; and they feared the king, for they saw the 'wisdom of God' was in him to better administer justice."

With Solomon's reign over Israel marked by his wisdom, the book's author writes, "And men of all nations, from all the kings of the earth who have heard of his wisdom, came to hear the wisdom of Solomon." Would it not be a wonderful, glorious day when "men of all nations" came to Judea to meet their wise king? The writers used such stories to invoke longing and pride among their roughed-up people, hoping to inspire them to find a leader other nations would respect.

Building was also a commonly revered quality for a king, and Solomon didn't disappoint. Chapter 6 has Solomon building a grand temple made of stone, the House of the Lord. The temple stands three stories high and includes a fifty-foot-long vestibule, or entrance, and several chambers. The walls and beams are made of prized cedar wood, the floors covered with cypress planks. The temple also includes a magnificent inner sanctuary as the "Most Holy Place," and the entire interior is cedar; "no stone was seen." The doors are made of olive wood, and the "whole temple he overlaid with gold." The project is said to have taken over eleven years to complete.

This is followed by Solomon building his own house, a project taking thirteen years. It is a raising "fit for a king." Solomon's building does not end here. He builds the "House of the Forest of Lebanon" and the "Hall of Pillars," both made with "costly stone."

The occupying Babylonians had destroyed the Judeans' temple long before in Jerusalem. One asks in regard to Solomon's grand architectural and building skills, "who among you can build another of even more grandeur?" *Think big*, thinks Solomon! *If you can't build big, at least dream big.* By emphasizing Solomon's prowess in regard to his wisdom and particularly his building and construction skills, were the biblical writers using this story as yet another example of leadership that potential leaders in waiting may inspire to? If one were to organize a grand construction project aimed at erecting an impressive edifice, would that not be an example of leadership great enough to inspire his fellow people to follow him into a common future?

As the story progresses, Solomon's wealth and fame grow large, and eventually "King Solomon surpassed all the kings of the earth in riches and wisdom." This is another, tiny little example of the beautiful, inspiring fiction the biblical writers set out to construct. One time ago, according to the tale, the Judeans' king had been richer and wiser than "all the kings of the earth."

As this captivating story proceeds, word of Solomon reaches the ear of the Queen of Sheba, who has to see for herself the wealth Solomon has obtained. "She came to Jerusalem with a very great retinue, with camels that bore spices, very much gold and precious stones ..." and tells Solomon, "your wisdom and prosperity exceed the fame of which I heard."

But Solomon has flaws that impair his leadership, and those Judean leaders in waiting must heed such flaws and their consequences. It is Solomon's love for many foreign women, including the daughter of the pharaoh, that begins his undoing—his Achilles' heel, so to speak, but a good hundred years before the legend of Achilles had been conceived.

The Lord has warned Solomon, "You shall not intermarry with [other nations]," but Solomon gave no regard to the Lord's urging. "For Solomon went after Ashtoreth, the goddess of the Sidonians, and after Milcom the abomination of the Ammonites." Despite all his wisdom, worshipping other gods brought Solomon down. Solomon's turning away from the Lord for riches, foreign women, and Ashtoreth was too much for Him to overlook. Chapter 11:11 reads, "Therefore the Lord said to Solomon, Because you have done this, and not kept My covenant and My statutes, which I have commanded you, I will surely tear your kingdom away from you and give it to your servant." However, the Lord tells Solomon He will not take it from him, but from his son, whose "yoke" will be "made heavy." At the end of the chapter, the wise but foolish Solomon dies and is buried in the "City of David his father."

The story of Solomon, son of David, is the story of a very wise man who was handed the keys to the kingdom but failed in the eyes of the Lord despite his great wisdom. His downfall was attributed in part to the abominations of the many foreign women taken for wives and the great wealth he acquired, but mostly came from turning away from the Lord and toward Ashtoreth. This has been an important theme of all the biblical writers of Genesis through Kings. Among their biggest fears was that the Judean people would be "seduced" by the gods and cultures of the surrounding city-states and disappearing into those cultures. The biblical writers knew their people and their civilization were hanging by a thread; if the Hebrews could be convinced to worship their *own* Lord, this could help hold them together.

The writers knew all too well that the people needed a good leader to rise up among them. Wisdom, more so than charisma, was one important quality. But another of perhaps even more importance was the ability to mission the "Lord of Israel" among the people. Effectively doing so would have long-term consequences. Instilling belief and trust in the Hebrews' own caring and everlasting Lord was essential for this outcome to occur. In the writers' opinion, someone who could do this well would make a good king. A very wise, savvy, and intelligent man who did not keep the Lord in his heart, such as Solomon, may bring immediate relief but could ultimately be a disaster for the Jewish people, imperiling their chances for a long, enduring future guided by the steady hand of their own Lord. The biblical writers put their highest hopes on the bonding power of religion to carry their people into the future. As these writers had endured incompetent secular leaders who led them straight into their exile, it's easy to see why. A Solomon-like leader wasn't the answer; this was made clear given the examples tagging poor leadership tendencies and practices.

As the book of Kings narrative continues, Solomon's son Rehoboam becomes king after Solomon's death and reigns over the Southern Kingdom of Judea while the now-long-gone northern kingdom of Israel is ruled by Jeroboam. Chapter 13 promptly removes all doubt of who between them will emerge the better King: Rehoboam. This would not have surprised those listening to this story, given the then well-known event of the demise of the northern kingdom of Israel.

Colorful anecdotes, prophecies, and imagery including a lion sitting over but not eating a corpse carry the kingship debacle of Jeroboam's reign into chapter 14. Here, the Lord vents his anger with Jeroboam's failures in no uncertain terms, which may leave one wondering why the all-knowing Lord chose him in the first place—but that is beside the point. The prophet Ahijah obediently delivers the Lord's words to the disguised wife of Jeroboam, who is purposely pretending to be "another woman" given the bad news she expects to receive. Regarding her husband, she's instructed to "Go tell Jeroboam, Thus says the Lord God of Israel: Because I exalted you from among the people, and made you ruler over My people Israel, and tore the kingdom away from the house of David, and gave it to you; and yet you have not been as My servant David who kept My commandments …" Furthermore, she's told to say "… but you have done more evil than all before you, for you have gone and made for yourself other gods and molded images to provoke Me to anger, and have cast Me behind your back …"

This reminds us again that the biblical writers often repeated the themes they felt most important, with the intended goal of helping the greater audience absorb their most important messages. Invoking disdain over "other gods and molded images" as often as they did underscores the biblical writers' seemingly greatest fear: the allure of the cultures and gods of the many surrounding and prosperous city-states, especially given the dire conditions of Jerusalem during the years of the exile. Even today, many conservative and Orthodox Jewish elders warn about the same. How easy is it for the educated and independently minded Jews schooled at any number of great universities to assimilate with and settle down into American or European societies? How easy is it for them to intermarry, prosper, and live worldly lives among everyone else? People are people, and people do human things, be it in ancient Israel or modern America.

But this didn't stop the biblical writers from trying—actually, the biblical project is the most determined effort toward unity ever recorded in the long history of the Jewish people. Such an effort had been undertaken for good reason, as pointed out; these were no ordinary times for the Jewish civilization. They were desperate times that required desperate measures. And it was this desperation and the writers' limited options that brought the Bible into existence.

1 Kings 14 finds the Lord disappointed over His concerns for the Southern Kingdom of Judah too, where Rehoboam reigns.

"Now Judah did evil in the sight of the Lord, and they provoked Him to jealousy with their sins which they committed, more than all that their fathers had done. For they also built for themselves high places, sacred pillars, and wooden images on every high hill and under every green tree. And there were also perverted persons in the land. They did according to all the abominations of the nations which the Lord had cast out before the children of Israel."

(In subsequent translations of the Bible, the word *sodomy* was often used as translation for the Hebrew word *qedeshim*, or those practicing sodomy and prostitution in religious rituals, referred to here as "perverted.")

"And there was war between Rehoboam and Jeroboam all their days until Rehoboam was buried with his fathers." Jeroboam lives on in disgrace before the eyes of the Lord and is followed by the reigns of Abijam, Asa, Nadab, and Baasha. Next come Elah, Zimri, Omri, and the slightly more remarkable Ahab, son of Omri, who also does evil in the sight of the Lord. He and his conniving wife serve Baal—a big no-no. Her name, Jezebel, lived on to become a popular, defining noun. The Lord had Jezebel eaten by dogs at "the wall of Jezreel" and blamed her for "stirring up" Ahab.

The many references to Baal in the first book of Kings suggest that the Phoenician god may very well have been worshipped abundantly by many Judeans during the time the Bible was written. Warnings intended to turn the Judeans' faith away from Baal and "molded images of wood or stone" are found throughout the books of Kings, especially in 1 Kings. If the writers couldn't reach out from exile and convince their people to worship the Hebrew Lord instead of Baal, their hopes of keeping the Jewish people together and united would be severely, if not critically, compromised—especially considering their lot following the defeat, occupation, and exile of the Judeans at the hand of Babylon.

In the book's final chapter—more specifically, 22:17—is found a single sentence that brightly illuminates the collective view of all the biblical writers involved in this heroic effort as they cast their gaze toward Israel. The words were spoken by a messenger: "I saw all Israel scattered on the mountains, as sheep that have no shepherd."

The second book of Kings seamlessly carries forward the writers' gallant effort to bring a shepherd to the land. This suggests that the books of Kings, like the books of Samuel, had been written as one book but divided in two so as to accommodate the volume limitations of the scrolls.

2 Kings continues with the description of yet more kings of Israel and Judea—some good, many bad. Those who kept the "commandments of the Lord" were good kings; those who did not were bad kings. This same, familiar story is told again and again in more than one book for the hitherto-stated reason.

These kings set many examples. The bad kings' defining fault usually was worshipping Baal and Ashtoreth or making carved images out of wood and stone. One exception was Jehoram, son of Ahab, who is king of the northern kingdom of Israel. He does "evil in the sight of the Lord … but not like his father and mother; for he put away the sacred pillar of Baal …" His "wickedness" came from persisting "in the sins of Jereboam," who "made Israel sin …"

Like the books before it, 2 Kings uses captivating storytelling and inspirational anecdotes to entertain as well as instruct. Foremost are the works of the miracle-making prophet Elijah, a mysterious "man of God." He was "A hairy man wearing a leather belt around his waist." Elijah heals a man once stricken with leprosy by having him "dipped seven times in the Jordan … and his flesh was restored like the flesh of a little child, and he was clean." When a man chopping a tree loses his borrowed iron ax head in the water, this mysterious "man of God" throws a stick in the water where the ax head fell, "and he made the iron float." In earlier verses, Elijah fills a valley with water, but not from rain, and heals a dying child by putting his mouth, eyes, and hands on the child's mouth, eyes, and hands. For the down and out, stories such as these certainly had them believing, wishing, and hoping for a few miracles of their own. The powerful human emotions of inspiration and hope could get them through another day.

The prophet also aided an indebted woman by turning one jar of oil into many, allowing her to pay her debts and purchase enough food for her starving sons. The haunting dread from debt and poverty would have permeated the Judean community during these desperate times. Such miraculous acts suggest that Elijah may have been the prototype for the Jesus character, despite the name "Jesus" being Greek for Joshua. When the books of Kings were being written, the Babylonians were at the Hebrews' gates. When the Gospels of Christ were written, the Romans were at their gates.

Although it is an accounting of the many kings who ruled over both kingdoms, Judea and Israel, the books of Kings's primary focus was to again discourage the worship of Baal and Ashtoreth while promoting the worship of the Hebrews' own Lord. With few exceptions, the numerous kings that come and go throughout the twenty-four chapters are either faithful to the Lord and His commandments, or faithful toward Baal. The latter are bad kings; the former are good kings.

The writer's contempt for Baal is seen throughout the book. In chapter 10 is a good example. Verse 18 reads, "Ahab served Baal a little, Jehu will serve him much." Jehu announces he'll make a great sacrifice to Baal "and all the worshipers of Baal came. But Jehu acted deceptively, with the intent of destroying the worshipers of Baal." Having gathered them in the temple of Baal, Jehu has them all killed. "Then they broke down the sacred pillar of Baal, and tore down the temple of Baal and made it a refuse dump to this day." In chapter 11, we read of the same fate for another temple of Baal. The display of so much contempt for Baal indicates how imperative it was in the minds of the biblical writers to worship the Hebrew Lord for the sake of unity.

2 Kings 10:32 is worth noting too. "In those days the Lord began cutting off parts of Israel …" As previously pointed out, the northern kingdom of Israel had vanished long before the biblical writers sat down to their task in 562 BCE. Saving the Southern Kingdom was imperative for these great patriots of Judea, who wrote the Bible to save Judaism and its culture, customs, and traditions from slowly evaporating. The Jewish temple in Jerusalem, an important symbol of a distinct people, had been destroyed by the Babylonians; their people's wealth had been plundered and their leaders exiled.

Chapter 12 illuminates the biblical writers' valid concerns over how best to counter Babylonian designs for the destruction of a united and national Jewish people. The rebuilding of the temple, the symbol of Judaism and center of its theocratic governing body, was a matter of high concern for the preservation of the Jewish people. Raising money (taxing) for the specific purpose of rebuilding the temple was encouraged by the biblical writers, as found in this chapter. More important, the restoration of a governing body that would naturally arise from the undertaking of a large building project and the subsequent administration of the temple would help restore much-needed leadership among the desperate Judean people.

A grand and comprehensive design it was that arose from the heroic biblical writers' minds. Their instructions for raising money from the community are found in 12:4–16. They read in part:

All the money of the dedicated gifts that are brought into the house of the Lord—each man's census money, each man's assessment money—and all the money a man purposes in his heart to bring into the house of the Lord … let the priests each take it themselves form his constituency; and let them repair the damages of the temple ...

King Jehoash asks, "Why have you not repaired the damages of the Temple? Now therefore, do not take more money from your constituency, but deliver it for repairing the damages of the temple."

... Then they gave the money, which had been apportioned, into the hands of those that did the work, who had the oversight of the house of the Lord; and they paid it to the carpenters and builders who worked on the house of the Lord, and to masons and stone cutters, and for buying timber hewn stone ...

Items of gold and silver "they gave to the workmen, and they repaired the house of the Lord with it." The temple symbolized the Jewish people, and the temple's destruction was yet another big obstruction to an enduring future for the Jewish people.

The following chapters tell of Elisha's death and the reigns of still more bad kings, who leave their struggling brothers and sisters in Jerusalem to blame for the mess they're in. With 2 Kings 17:19–23, the writer returns to the lost kingdom of Israel once again. In part, it reads,

Also Judah did not keep the commandments of their Lord ... but walked in the statures of Israel which they made. And the Lord rejected all the descendants of Israel, afflicted them, and delivered them into the hands of plunderers, until He had cast them from His sight. For He tore Israel from the house of David ... Israel was carried away from their own land to Assyria, as it is to this day.

In the biblical writers' minds, this was the preferred way to explain the loss of the Northern Kingdom of Israel, rather than admitting to the truth—that the lost tribe had been defeated by an enemy and simply blended into the more promising surrounding cultures through marriage and economy. Once those of the northern kingdom learned the language of the surrounding culture, that was that.

As pointed out more than once, this exact same fate was besieging the Southern Kingdom of Judea at the time. This obviously was *the* fear harbored within the writers' hearts and minds. Preventing the disappearance of the Judean culture was clearly the goal of their large, costly, and grand biblical writing project.

In chapter 19:10–11, we read, "Jerusalem shall not be given into the hand of the king of Assyria. Look! You have heard what the kings of Assyria have done to all lands by utterly destroying them; and shall you be delivered?" Chapter 19 implores the people to embrace their Lord. In verse 32, the poem reads,

Therefore thus says the Lord concerning the king of Assyria … He shall not come into this city, Nor shoot an arrow there, Nor come before it with a shield, Nor build a siege mound against it. By the way that he came [from Babylon?] By the same shall he return: And he shall not come into this city, says the Lord. For I will defend this city, to save it for My own sake and for my servant David's sake.

Eventually the subterfuge is dropped, and the writer bravely places his pen directly upon Babylon and Nebuchadnezzar himself. This may very well be directly linked to the death of Nebuchadnezzar in 562 BCE, the year the exiled biblical writers likely sat down to their task of composing Genesis through Kings II. This event alone may have been the catalyst that launched their biblical writing project. A lot of consideration and thought regarding the compositions certainly would have preceded their sitting down to this enormous and risky task.

Another possible dating scenario may show the biblical project beginning a year or two before 562 BCE and concluding around 562 BCE. The seemingly sudden and direct emphasis on King Nebuchadnezzar toward the end of Kings II may indicate that he had been alive during much of the time Genesis–Kings II was being written. This may explain why the death of this towering figure suddenly appears in the last few chapters of the second book of Kings, which concludes the biblical project's story. Then again, perhaps not. Ponder this question for yourself; it's interesting to consider.

2 Kings 20:17–18 reads,

Behold, the days that are coming when all that is in your house, and what your fathers have accumulated until this day, shall be carried to Babylon; nothing shall be left, says the Lord. And they shall take away some of your sons that descend from you, whom you will beget; and they shall be eunuchs in the palace of the king of Babylon.

This is a very direct and strong warning, and is followed with more warnings against worshipping the foreign gods Baal and Asherah; making wood carvings; practicing soothsaying; practicing witchcraft; "and consulting spiritists and mediums."

In the book's closing two chapters, the writer provides his specific, targeted audience with a recent and more reliable historical account of the real king of Babylon, Nebuchadnezzar, and what was done to Judea by the hands of the Chaldeans— all slightly safer to write given that Nebuchadnezzar was now deceased. "And Nebuchadnezzar king of Babylon came against the city, and his servants were besieging it … Also, he carried into captivity all Jerusalem; all the captains and all the mighty men of valor, ten thousand captives, and all the craftsmen and smiths. None remained but the poorest people of the land." It was solely for these poverty-stricken and vulnerable people, "the poorest people of the land," that the Bible, Genesis through Kings II, was written.

In the book's final four verses, the Babylonian king releases Jehoiachin, the king of Judah, from prison but holds him in house arrest. So Jehoiachin changes from his prison garment, and he eats bread regularly before the king all the days of his life. "And as for his provisions, there was a regular ration given him by the king, a portion for each day, all the days of his life."

With those words, the biblical work of the writers is brought to an end. They are all dead now, but for their living remains this. Bravo!

CHAPTER 16

# Genesis through Kings II

The exile in 586 BCE of the Jewish upper classes left their people's prospects for survival as a culture very bleak, and their futures even as individuals in dire straits. Jerusalem is situated between the River Jordan and the magnificent Mediterranean Sea. Just north was Phoenicia and Tyre, a port city and center of trade on the west shore of the Mediterranean, halfway between Egypt to the south and Ugarit to the north. At the time, Canaan was at the center of the universe, so to speak. It would be an easy place for one to get caught up in his own economy and adopt a "to each his own" attitude even without the Judeans' society in disarray, their temple in ruins, and their leaders exiled far away.

The biblical writers and scribes, on the other hand, were bound and determined not to let that happen. Their desperate attempt to save their culture and society from oblivion rested only upon ink, papyrus, and their wisdom. Little did they know that as large and ambitious as the Genesis–Kings II writing project was, their work would ultimately become something much grander, and reach way beyond their original intent.

As we look back, we see now how the biblical writers' work would help shape world history over the millennia. It would spark divisions and wars. It would create venerable institutions that wielded great power and influence often rivaling that of even the strongest kings and states.

Yet, the Bible's original purpose, while noble, was particularly narrow: to keep the Jewish underclasses united as a people and prevent the cultural demise that had befallen the Judeans' northern brothers and sisters in Israel. This brings up an important question: did the Bible work as the writers had intended it to?

The answer to this question appears to be an obvious yes. Not only did the Bible unite the Jewish people then, but it has also held them united ever since, or so it unequivocally appears. But could this long-distance writing project of a few copies of instructional and inspirational print on scrolls have achieved the writers' goals had it not been for subsequent and significant historical events? One such event was the rise of Cyrus the Great, who founded the emerging Persian Empire in 539 BCE after conquering the Babylonians and their wealthy state. His subsequent edict in 537 BCE freed the Hebrews from Babylonia's control and allowed them to return to Jerusalem and rebuild their temple. Could the Bible alone have ensured the success of the Jewish people without Cyrus's edict? Maybe yes, maybe no. The question deserves its due respect from every perspective.

Unsurprisingly, despite Cyrus's edict, nearly all surviving members of these generations remained in what many accounts described as the most beautiful and opulent city in the ancient Near East, Babylon, home of the magnificent Ishtar Gate, the colossal Etemenanki (more popularly known as the Tower of Babel) and the Hanging Gardens of Babylon, one of the Seven Wonders of the World. Who among these post-exiled generational inhabitants would want to go back to the dregs of Jerusalem in the aftermath of its Babylonian occupation? There were not many. By most accounts, only a very small percentage chose to do exactly that.

Those contemplating a return to Jerusalem and Judea must have wondered what awaited them there. Given the destruction of the temple and the dreadful living conditions, many had to have been deeply concerned about what would remain of their society upon their return. The worshipping of Baal was an obvious worrisome matter for the returnees, and for good reason. Younger Hebrew generations were always at risk of being absorbed into the Phoenician culture, be it by marriage or choice, especially during the decades of exile. This was clearly an obvious fear of the biblical writers and the exiled returnees they inspired, as illustrated by the many references and warnings against Baal worshipping in the biblical books they authored. How tempting and easy would it have been for young Hebrew adults to get swept up by the Phoenician culture and society, where opportunities and seduction always loomed? In contrast, little promise remained of the shattered Hebrew society in Jerusalem at the time. How close had the Judean society come to reaching the point of no return as specifically prescribed by the hand of Nebuchadnezzar and the Babylonians with the exile of their leaders? Was anything was left standing of the Judeans' preexilic cultural institutions, let alone anything worth saving? From most contemporary perspectives, the future of the Jewish people may very well have seemed doomed.

Standing between this deep divide and extreme consequence, along with the Bible, was King Cyrus's edict in 537 BCE granting the exiled Hebrew descendants the opportunity to return to Jerusalem and bring with them a few additional copies of Genesis–Kings II. It's possible some of the returnees hoped to reunite with family members or friends, but with nearly fifty years having passed since the exile and limited contact between the two groups, this motivation seems very unlikely, if not nonexistent. The only reason one can imagine for the people to leave behind their familiar routine and comfortable lives in Babylon and return to Jerusalem or Judah was the travelers' dedicated commitment to their heritage and the struggling Hebrew community still standing in Jerusalem and Judea. Those who chose to return under these pretenses were the truest of patriots deeply committed to a very noble cause—that being nothing short of saving their own people from extinction at great sacrifice to their own unselfish selves.

First among this small number of Hebrews who chose to return and were able enough to make the long trek back to their pre-exiled home (now promoted as the promised land) had to have included those associated with or deeply motivated by the biblical writing project. Most, if not all, of these compatriots would comprise the surviving and able-bodied biblical authors, their assistants, their wives, and at least some of their immediate family members and close relatives, advisers, and friends. Very few descendants of those exiled fifty years prior would otherwise be impelled to leave Babylon or pulled by opportunity in Judea to take up stakes.

The few associating around the Bible who did return were probably different in several ways from the many left behind, as one could easily imagine. Having lived in Babylon for the past fifty years (which in some cases amounted to their entire lives), these visitors would find the Judean culture, religion, politics, and a host of other customs, viewpoints, and attitudes to be nearly foreign. Of course, Jewish traditions and stories of old would likely have been passed down from parents to siblings living in Babylonia following the exile. Nonetheless,

Judea was hundreds of miles away from Babylon—an arduous trek in those days.

This leads one to believe that those who chose to return did so because they were Jewish. They were not assimilated enough with Babylonia, unlike the overwhelming percentage of the exiled Hebrews and their offspring who chose to remain there. It was they, the returnees, who would ultimately play an important role in events that would influence world history for thousands of years to come—and still counting. The returnees brought Judaism back to their homeland. Those among them who had undertaken scholarly work, scribing, and advocacy of the Bible would be of paramount service to future generations of Jews.

Among the returnees were also those holding onto a deep desire to rebuild the temple destroyed by the Babylonians. Not long after their return, work began on the rebuilding of the temple, an edifice of important symbolic interest for all the faithful Hebrews. This second temple was maintained over the ages. Having been structurally reinforced in the first century BCE by Herod the Great, the second temple would ultimately stand for six hundred years before its destruction by the occupying Romans in 70 CE. The temple institutionalized Judaism, and its presence played a crucial role in holding Judaic culture and society together.

Despite the representative and institutional importance of the second temple, and with the continued tedious reproduction of the biblical books Genesis through Kings II by scribes, history failed to mention much of the Hebrews for several centuries to come. Overshadowed by those cast from the great states of Mesopotamia, Assyria, Egypt, Babylonia, Phoenicia, Persia, Greece, and Rome, the nonbiblical literary, technological, socioeconomic, and political remains of the ancient Hebrew civilization are essentially nonexistent in comparison.

If it were not for the Bible, how much historical mention would have followed the Hebrews? Their early sheepherding economy and social tribal and extended family tradition veered away from the formation of city-states. The scattered Hebrew settlements found within the regions of other states that had taken hold early in the Hebrews' history set the pattern of diaspora away from an ancestral homeland. Although the city of Jerusalem was founded around 4000 BCE, the large concentrations of ancient Hebrews that began to form ad hoc in Jerusalem and surrounding areas around 1100–1000 BCE would eventually associate the city indelibly with the Jewish people, and much later with the Bible.

After this review, it does appear that the Bible and Cyrus's edict together played the crucial hand that preserved the Judaic culture and society throughout the ages while history's greatest and most mighty Western ancient civilizations, including the likes of Phoenicia, Persia, Greece, and Rome, all fell. Or, was the biblical writers' fear of the Hebrews' dissolution unwarranted? To date, our best academic and archaeological evidence reveals that the Hebrew or Judaic people have been around for about 3,250 years and counting. Only the ancient Southern Mesopotamian continuous civilization that thrived for about 3,900 years and the ancient Egyptian civilization that endured for 5,642 years have reigned on earth for a longer period than the ancient Hebrews and their Judaic descendants. If not for the Bible, what else may have played a role in such a long life span?

One consideration was the Hebrews' lack of their own strong state and territorial boundaries throughout most of their history. During their earlier history, the Hebrew people settled an area about five hundred miles long and up to two hundred miles wide along the western coast of, and inlands off, the Mediterranean Sea. They were divided into two kingdoms,

Israel in the north and Judea in the south—a division that apparently weakened them. Eventually, the northern tribes of Israel disappeared amid other cultures and were later referred to as the lost tribes of Israel, as mentioned earlier. The missing northern tribes were presumably absorbed into the surrounding settlements through intermarriage, and perhaps more so by the popular embrace of a foreign culture whose customs became familiar, routine, and practical. Over time they and all subsequent generations became aggregately and completely assimilated.

In the south, the Hebrew populations were less scattered and more concentrated, especially in settlements off the southwestern coast of the Mediterranean Sea. Archaeology has uncovered a few ancient Hebrew settlements near or within the territorial jurisdictions of others, presumably populated mostly by migrant Hebrews looking for work as economic conditions dictated. Being a peaceful, un-intrusive people respectful of others' traditions and customs while also skilled, talented and hardworking, the ancient Hebrews often, begrudgingly or not, complimented and contributed to their host's economy. The Hebrews' presence was tolerated, but many of the people they labored for looked down upon them with degrees of contempt. Why? One can only shrug. Because the majority populations were not threatened by them, and their little personal and collective wealth was not worth fighting or conquering them for, they were generally left alone.

A comparative large concentration of Hebrews did form in the city of Jerusalem and the area surrounding it, known as Judea. Consequently, not long after Judea became in essence a small vassal state of Persia in 539 BCE, the Hebrews came to be called "Jews," short for "Judean," and to this day prefer to be recognized by that term.

Persia's approximate two-hundred-year period of hegemony

over its vast territorial conquests, including Judea, is characterized as one of temperance, accommodation, and relative prosperity. With prosperity came stability, contentment, and peace. As the Jewish population became more affluent and hunger less of a concern, the finer things in life became more accessible for many, including the opportunity to learn how to read and write. Unfortunately, ancient Jerusalem was never known for its libraries. Very few scrolls containing literary prose existed, and what did exist was written by other civilizations, including Egypt and Mesopotamia, as illustrated in Part One of this book.

Most writing in Jerusalem was relegated to economic record keeping. Then and there, as is now and here, the extra time given over by a more abundant food supply provided economic opportunities. If accumulating money and commodity during these prosperous times was the order of the day, using valuable time to learn how to read and write would seem downright foolish for many. But for more than a few Jews, literacy was deemed a worthwhile, if not divine, pursuit. Given what we know today, many Jewish men and women living way back then decided to learn how to read and write. The Bible played a large part in this, as did other literature.

Despite the lack of large amounts of Judaic literary text in Jerusalem during the start of Persian hegemony under Cyrus the Great, there were certainly some original texts of national origin to be found that could be tediously reproduced; the most significant of these, of course, were the now-famous books of Genesis through Kings II. Those books were written by Jews for Jews in their own Hebrew alphabet.

The stage was set for the biblical literary project to grow. During the two-hundred-year Persian period (539–332 BCE) and the following Hellenistic period (332–200), many enjoyed general prosperity, extra money, and more free time. Of greater historical significance there was the inspiration that flowed forth from Genesis–Kings II that encouraged many others to take up the pen. Nearly all the Hebrew biblical books added to Genesis–Kings II were added during the Persian and Hellenistic periods of Judaic history. The one exception, the book of Daniel, was written around 167 BCE, during the Hasmonean period (200–63 BCE). Through time, these books all joined with Genesis through Kings II to form the Hebrew Bible, also known somewhat incorrectly as the Old Testament.

The writing of the New Testament's first books, including the Gospels of Jesus, the books Matthew, Mark, and Luke, is estimated to have begun around 40–60 CE and concluded around 80 CE.

Little did the biblical writers of Genesis–Kings II realize how great the impact their work would have on world history. It's been nearly 2,600 years since they completed their work. Their Bible has since become the biggest publishing event in world history.

CHAPTER 17

# History Repeats

An honest refrain we often hear is, "History repeats itself." It is easy to explain why. People are people, and people do people things over and over again. This notion seems to epitomize Jewish history from its beginning to end.

In 332 BCE, under the leadership of the Greek-speaking Macedonian Alexander the Great, the Persian Empire toppled under the growing influence of Greece. Alexander and his Macedonians imported and installed a hybrid but extraordinary Greek cultural heritage that thrived, ushering in the glorious Hellenistic period. Alexander's prosperous empire would last for 123 years.

After Alexander's death in 323 BCE, various competing generals wrestled for control and influence, leading to that ever- and forever-long trend in Judaism that we see to this day. Many upper classes of Jews adopted several Greek customs and philosophies, essentially becoming Greek, or Hellenized. Many other Jews looking to advance themselves chose likewise, and why not? The Greek civilization originating just across the other side of the Mediterranean was something to behold and marvel, not only by the Jews but many others as well. There was nothing like it, and Ancient Greece is still revered to this day. Who could fault them?

The few biblical books written during this period, particularly Ecclesiastes and Song of Songs, clearly reflect a Greek incursion into the Jewish mind of the upwardly mobile and the upper class itself. Its Hellenistic influence is easily recognized. In the opening chapters of Ecclesiastes, we read,

Vanity of vanities says the preacher; Vanity of vanities, all is vanity. What profit has a man from all his labor in which he toils under the sun? One generation passes away, and another generation comes; but the earth abides forever. ... For in much wisdom is much grief, and he who increases knowledge increases sorrow. ... I searched in my heart how to gratify my flesh with wine, while guiding my heart with wisdom, and how to lay hold on folly, till I might see what was good for the sons of men to under heaven all the days of their lives.

In chapter 3 are the phrases much more remembered today as lyrics found in a popular rock song recorded during the conflicted years of the late 1960s and early 1970s than as part of the book of Ecclesiastes: "To everything there is a season, a time for every purpose under heaven: A time to be born, and a time to die; a time to plant, a time to kill, a time to heal ... A time to weep, and a time to laugh ... A time to love and a time to hate ... A time for war and a time for peace ..."

Certainly appropriate were these ancient lyrics during the divisive times brought about by America's war with Vietnam, when they came to be planted in our memories and our hearts by this popular song that sold many vinyl 45- and 33-rpm records. Recorded by Peter, Paul, and Mary (familiar biblical names), the song saw many hours of playing time on AM and FM radio stations whose transmitted sound waves flowed into countless homes and automobiles throughout much of the world.

Song of Songs is flush with eroticism rivaling that found in Greek literature and art. In chapter 7, we read,

How beautiful are your feet in sandals, O prince's daughter! The curves of your thighs are like jewels, the work of the hands of a skillful workman. Your navel is a rounded goblet; it lacks no blended beverage. Your waist is a heap of wheat set about with lilies. Your two breasts are like two fawns, twins of a gazelle. Your neck is like an ivory tower ... O love, with your delights! This stature of yours is like a palm tree, and your breasts like its clusters ... Let now your breasts be like clusters of the vine, the fragrance of your breath like apples, and the roof of your mouth like the best wine.

Verses such as these could lead one to wonder if at least a few Jewish parents became a bit concerned about these racy lyrics during the golden times when Athens reigned. Yet, such words found their way into the Bible—granted, they weren't the words of the first biblical writers, but ultimately inspired by them.

After a long lull, times were changing again. After the Seleucids of Syria took control of Judea around 200 BCE, their attempt to unify their Jewish subjects with an encompassing Greek Hellenistic culture eventually provoked resistance from the more conservative and Orthodox groups within the Judaic population. For these more conservative Jews, "breasts like clusters" shouldn't necessarily be the 'order up' of the day. Although tolerant and understanding in many regards including love, sex, and intellectual and philosophical pursuits, the Orthodox parties drew a line in the sand when it came to traditions at the heart of Jewish identity, such as circumcision and the temple sacrifices abundantly emphasized in Genesis through Kings II.

The Maccabee rebellion in 168 BCE, sparked by the desecration of the temple at the hand of the Seleucids, was a case in point. The Seleucid ruler, Antiochus Epiphanes, attempted to impose total Hellenization upon the Jews and succumbed to their rebellion, ultimately liberating Jerusalem and leaving Greek influences checked. The Jewish festival customarily held in December, known as Hanukkah, or dedication, marks this very event. For the next hundred years, Judea was ruled by the Hasmonean dynasty, descendants of Judas Maccabeus.

At the time of the Maccabee rebellion in 168 BCE, all the biblical books of the Jewish canon and Old Testament had been written for some time except the last, the book of Daniel.

Daniel, as mentioned, was written around 167 BCE, only one year after the Maccabee rebellion began. It's a very intriguing work. Daniel is remembered for his great wisdom and visions, but the book curiously concerns itself with Nebuchadnezzar and the Babylonians, with no mention of the current Maccabee rebellion that has risen up in opposition to the Seleucids and their king, Epiphanes. Upon closer examination, the book's author may have intentionally employed subterfuge to confuse and underhand his Seleucid overseers.

It is interesting to take special note of the book of Daniel's harkening back some four hundred years to the time when Jerusalem had been occupied by the strong-armed power of Babylon, later ousted by Cyrus the Great of Persia. Daniel's mention of his own prosperity under the liberating King Cyrus in 6:28, and his earlier translation of the coded, and now famous refrain "handwriting on the wall" at the behest of King Belshazzar, which correctly predicts the king's own demise in chapter 5, has engaging and curious parallels with the Maccabees' desired doom for Epiphanes's designs for the complete Hellenization of the Jews. The book of Daniel's message appears intended to "foretell" Epiphanes's failure to

Hellenize the Jews (an undertaking that would have stripped them of their own unique identity) and the ultimate success of the Maccabee rebellion. It's quite curious, and could very likely be the fundamental purpose behind the book of Daniel. Again, we see how events have shaped the Bible.

However, Daniel didn't predict a crippling power struggle resembling civil war among the Hasmoneans and the consequent invasion of "the promised land" by the most powerful state of the time ever to emerge, the Roman Empire. Deep social and religious divisions among the Jews had Rome smelling blood in the water. The Romans' zeal for conquest brought Pompey's Roman legions into Jerusalem in 63 BCE, and their military victory over the city was swift and complete. Despite brave Judaic attempts to resist, and even braver outright rebellions against Roman rule by such groups as the Zealots, internal rivalries and the power of Rome dictated the course of Jewish history.

The last great rebellion against Roman occupation occurred in 132 CE after the Roman emperor Hadrian issued an edict against the practice he abhorred, circumcision. The rebellion was brutally squashed. Hadrian brought to Jerusalem a large population composed of foreign migrants who built a new city of Roman design on the heap of busted rock of that great and enduring ancient metropolis. Their final coup de grâce was to enhance the even-then-ancient city with numerous statues of Roman deities and symbols.

As for the significantly reduced population of Jews who managed to survive the Roman assault that came down upon them, they were not so much as even permitted to enter Jerusalem, the very city that had identified them for centuries. Most packed up what they could and headed out of the land they had occupied for 1,200 years. Off they went in many different directions, beginning yet another journey into an uncertain, uncompromising, and unpromising destiny. But history would offer a few surprises.

The Jews had appeared doomed by the hand of the marauding Sea Peoples, or Philistines, in the eleventh century BCE. They survived. After the northern kingdom of Israel disappeared around 722 BCE following incursions from Assyria, the same fate seemed certain to befall the Southern Kingdom of Judah. They survived. Crushed by Babylon in 605 BCE and again in 586 BCE and their leaders exiled, the Jews' desolation and ruin seemed complete. They survived. In 168 BCE, the Seleucids of Syria thought they could crush the Jews. They survived. In 132 CE, the Romans squashed the Jews, built a Roman city on top of Jerusalem, and renamed the Jews' land Syria Palestina—after the Philistines, no less. The Jews survived. Following their slaughter by the Romans, the fleeing Jews scattered far and wide around the globe in small communities, with each communal group eventually settling down somewhere and surviving.

The Bible neither created nor provided a state for the Jews. It did, however, establish a constitution of sorts that would help unite, govern, and guide their lives, a feat that ultimately played a leading role in unifying and preserving the Jewish people and their society through the ages, exactly as originally and specifically intended by the biblical writers. The biblical writings inspired hope and relief, their stories educated and entertained, and their laws advanced codes of conduct and suggested treatments for disease. The Bible established observances and holidays that helped bond and shape Jewish life and inspired future generations to add glorious prose to the tome.

Alongside the growth of the Jewish community ascended the rabbinic and clerical professions, coupled with their venerable institutions, the synagogue and the Christian churches that followed with the latter's embrace of both the Old Testament literature and future Jewish writings pertaining to a "Son of God," Jesus Christ. Together, the Old Testament and New Testament preserved and advanced biblical faith through the millennia into our present times.

For the greater part of the Jews' long and ongoing history, their Bible and traditions remained with them, as did their practice of circumcision, which eventually caught on among non-Jewish male populations who faithfully accepted the procedure as advocated by the books of Moses. Fortuitously broadened in scope and reach by Flavius Josephus's Greek translation, along with the subsequent Latin and King James English translations, the Bible would follow the Jews to their farthest reaches.

Several Jewish customs and practices beyond circumcision became embedded within many diverse populations. But it was the cohesive Genesis–Kings II "sacred" literature promoting a Lord of their very own and establishing the Jews as His chosen people—in addition to sharing some unique customs and practices, including celebratory observations, dietary laws, and circumcision—that most identified the Jewish people and held them together in an embrace.

Following the mass dispersion, or diaspora, from Judea that began after 135 CE, and the Jews' continued long, slow, and deliberate migration to other regions, the original Hebrew language was eventually lost among the many scattered Jewish populations in favor of their hosts' language, and their bloodlines were naturally altered.

It makes one wonder how the Jews managed to persevere despite many severe and varied challenges while all the other great ancient powers, including Greece and Rome, fell one after the other into extinction. Before holding up the Bible, more needs to be considered.

History has demonstrated a predictable pattern of the rise and fall of states. States rise, decline, and fall. A *state* can be defined as a changing but continuous governing body over an occupied territorial boundary, and seemingly destined to fall over various durations of time. But if there were no state to begin with, would there be a fall? Until 1948 CE, the Jews never had their own state, be it a city-state or otherwise. Although they lived under various governing units of one sort or another, they occupied areas that were also home to many others, including Jerusalem, which had been settled thousands of years before the Jews arrived. This non-state status may very well be the most significant consequential cause of the Jews' longevity.

Or could the cause be those first biblical writings, Genesis through Kings II, originally and specifically written to sustain their ancient civilization and society during the years of the Babylonian-imposed exile of their upper classes? Was the Bible so perfectly prescribed as to hold its future generations together as long as the Earth's humankind shall live?

While Genesis through Kings II was largely a code of laws, its inspirational storytelling was a masterful, imaginative work of fiction. Had it not been for the inspirational power of the writers' storytelling and its many make-believe components (which the wanting lower classes of less-educated compatriots were more inclined to be mindfully and emotionally moved by,) the biblical project may easily have failed. Images of a sea separating, the flow of the Jordan's river abruptly stopped, and the sun made standing still by the all-powerful and overwhelming hand of the Jews' own personal Lord provided what their people needed the most: hope and belief in one great sovereign whose heavenly strength would protect and shepherd them forward upon their path into their future.

By and through its fiction, the Bible has reached far and wide. It continues to excite deeply felt human emotions to this day, just as it did for the ancients. People are people who do people things be it those of yesteryear or today, and one such thing is to believe. In rapture we find bewitching enchantment. What's wrong with that?

CHAPTER 18

# What's Wrong with That?

That's a good and valid question. What *is* wrong with the Bible influencing modern cultures? Frankly, one can easily take a pretty good stab at this question. I remember listening to a fellow classmate lecture my roommate and me after a philosophy class we had just attended. He was a believer and argued that if he was wrong, so what? But if we were wrong in our beliefs, we would be doomed to spend eternity in hell. Our response was that we didn't know anything about hell, but we did know we had at least our one life on earth and we didn't want to live it believing in the wrong thing.

Modern science (of our day that is) precisely explains the omnipresent evolutionary processes governing all, including humankind itself. Powerful telescopes reveal a universe composed of billions, if not trillions, of galaxies, each composed of billions, if not trillions, of stars. Wherever we look, we're finding more and more planets revolving around more and more stars leaving many renowned scholars and simple observers alike convinced there are more planets than stars in the universe. In other words, it's very easy to conclude that our universe is teeming with life throughout, not just on earth.

The forces at work behind it all seem humanly incomprehensible in their great magnitudes and scopes. Is it time for us to spiritually evolve and move away from these ancient and superstitious Bible-based religions and begin to think outside the now-confining spiritual box they put us in? In our present times of rapidly advancing technology, new discoveries, and our greater understanding of natural science and the universe we live in, it seems inevitable that many will relentlessly continue to drift away from these outdated and superstitious laced biblical religious concepts as evidenced by declining membership in many churches and synagogues.

History is another subject I have read a lot of. It has taught me much too. Despite the original good and noble intentions of these great Abrahamic religions, they have brought down upon us seemingly never-ending wars, divisions, and conflicts that have spilled so much blood, hostility, and hate among us that I must ask, what on earth for? Have these religions also made us crazy? This endless bickering among Christians, Jews, and Muslims over religious convictions seems never to resolve itself, leading the sane among us to ask "For what?" We are all human, we are all inherently good, our bodies have the same anatomy, our bodies perform the physiology and we all strive to live satisfying and worthwhile lives.

I was just a twelve-year-old in my second semester of sixth grade when my teacher scolded another boy after a girl in our class complained that he had made fun of her because she was "Jewish." The fact that I made it to twelve without hearing this word "Jew" and recognizing it as a distinguishing trait for the first time made the boy's behavior perplexing. Her name was Sarah, and it just so happened I had a childish crush on her. She was a new student who had joined our class that January.

I thought she was the prettiest girl in the world. Later that day during recess, I told her I would punch Jared in the nose for hurting her feelings, and confessed to liking her. She smiled, took my hand, and asked if I would come over to her house after school and play with her. I did. Her mom looked like any other mom, her house like any other house, and she played as any others would play. I remember her mom was so nice and gave us sweets to share. Even though I was a boy who passionately played boy games and did boy things, for the first time I felt something new about girls, about her. We continued to find plenty of time to play with each other outside and at our homes.

The following year, we danced only with each other at our school's combined seventh- and eighth-grade dance. It was exciting. That same night, she told me she would be my girlfriend if I would be her boyfriend. I have never had an easier time before or since saying yes to a proposition. She kissed me that night, and I always remembered that as my first. It felt good.

I found myself heartbroken for the first time a year or so later when she told me with a tear in her eye that she was moving to New York. Hearing that wasn't a good feeling. With Sarah, I first felt the joy and hurt that could come from liking a girl especially a lot. I wish I hadn't lost the three or four letters she wrote me after leaving, and I can only hope Sarah didn't lose those I wrote her. As for her Jewishness, what the heck was that about? The fact that adults felt there was something different between me and Sarah because she was "Jewish" left me feeling something strange that I couldn't understand. I didn't get it. Why, I thought, could something so nothing divide us so much? Sarah was nice, and cool, and so pretty—wasn't that enough? It was for me, that much was certain.

As I continued on with high school, college, graduate school, and my adult professional life, I met and worked alongside many more Jews, and I'm sure Sarah met many more Christians. I have learned that some of those born Jewish believe a lot, some believe a little, some don't believe at all, and some believe in something other. I'm sure Sarah also learned that some born Christian believe a lot, some believe a little, some don't believe at all, and some believe in something other. Why there was a Christian-versus-Jewish thing—among "grown-ups" no less—was something I couldn't understand way back then as a twelve-year-old, and it still perplexes me today. Why should anyone care what another chooses to spiritually believe in? What's wrong with that?

I enjoyed the years of teaching that brought my professional life to a wonderful close, if for no other reason than being around children again and my fellow teachers who also wished to teach them well. (See "About the Author," which follows.) I was fortunate to have taught at two highly respected private prep schools, my last a Modern Orthodox Jewish school. I remember one day hearing a young fourteen-year-old girl in my eighth-grade science class remarking to her nearby friends saying "This Jew thing is stupid!" I covered my smile while thinking *if you really want stupid, check out the Christian thing.*

But that was a few years ago and counting. I have since actually sat down and read—*studied* is the better word—much of this extraordinary book called the Bible. Genesis through Kings II is indeed something very remarkable. This old science and chemistry guy humbly nods, hat in hand, with great respect toward those who wrote the Bible, a truly extraordinary body of work.

As for you, my readers, this is why the first books of the Bible were written and who they were written for. As for me, I can now look that precious fourteen-year-old girl in the eye and say, "No, this Jew thing isn't stupid. Actually it was smart—very smart." But I must also add and easily ask this. Observant Jews hold high and stand side-by-side with their biblical ancestors Abraham, Isaac, and Jacob. Many believe them to be the patriarchs of the Jewish people. But are these fictional characters their true patriarchs? Shouldn't their true patriarchs be the biblical writers of Genesis through Kings II themselves? The writers of Genesis through Kings II are the true and deserving heroes of this great and enduring people, if not their saviors.

# ABOUT THE AUTHOR

Allen Wright lives with his wife in his beautiful home state of Michigan, following a thirty-five-year professional career in Dallas, Texas. He graduated from the University of California–Santa Barbara in 1975 with a BA in history and earned a master's in public administration (MPA) at Southern Methodist University, Dallas, Texas, in 1978. His career path involved city management and private-sector landfill management followed by owning and operating a successful business in Dallas that he later sold. He then became a teacher of history, general science, and chemistry. Mr. Wright's work appeared in the respected academic journal *The Journal for Biblical Literature* (JBL) in the summer of 2009. He retired in June 2010 at the age of 57. Along with research and writing, Allen Wright enjoys reading, hiking, and swimming. Wright is also engaged in politics; he recently won a contested seat to serve on his city's school board and has been appointed to serve on important city commissions. He is known to play a good game of racquetball, a hobby that began while attending UCSB, and in high school was named an all-conference football player who also excelled at baseball. Despite his mother's best efforts, Wright was never into church. His spiritual search engines are propelled by the sciences.